TRUE &
FALSE
REVIVAL

ANDREW STROM

RevivalSchool

TRUE & FALSE REVIVAL

Copyright © 2008 by Andrew Strom. All rights reserved.

Published by: RevivalSchool
www.revivalschool.com

Wholesale distribution by Lightning Source, Inc.

*Scripture taken from the New King James Version®. Copyright © 1982
by Thomas Nelson, Inc. Used by permission. All rights reserved.*

[Sometimes the KJV is also quoted].

ISBN-13: 978-0-9799073-1-9

ISBN-10: 0-9799073-1-4

1. Prophets -- History   2. Revivals

CONTENTS

CHAPTER ONE

WHY I LEFT THE PROPHETIC MOVEMENT

Let me start by saying that I always had high hopes for the Prophetic movement – that it would return to its original calling of preaching against lukewarmness and exhorting the church to repentance. (For isn't that what real prophets do?) But even at the height of my involvement, I could never work out why the modern 'Prophetic' seemed so un-prophet-like in this way.

I would read the history of Revivals and see that true Revival has always had the CROSS and REPENTANCE at its heart – and I couldn't understand why these things seemed so lacking in a movement that claimed the name "Prophetic".

Now, before I go any further, let me state that, to this day, I am still a strong Spirit-filled, tongues-speaking Christian. My involvement with the Prophetic movement goes back to 1993. (In fact, most of the leaders mentioned in this book, such as Todd Bentley, Patricia King, Bob Jones, Paul Cain, Mike Bickle, John Paul Jackson, etc, all have major involvement with this movement). Sadly, the Prophetic became one of the main "carriers" for the bizarre baggage that has attached itself to Charismatic Christianity over the last 15 years or so, and I found I could no longer remain.

I have been a writer and speaker on Revival for many years, and our ministry was based out of Kansas City itself for 2 ½ years. But in November 2004 while we were still living in that city, I felt compelled to publicly cut off all ties with the modern Prophetic in a way that was so public and final that it seemed to send shockwaves through the movement. In fact, my leaving caused a far greater outcry than my participation ever had. The fact was I could no longer stomach what was going on. I could no longer play any part in it at all. Just a few weeks earlier, Paul Cain, the man regarded by many as the 'father' of this movement, had been publicly exposed as having fallen into serious sin. (He issued his own confession in early 2005). But it wasn't the fall of Paul Cain that sent me over the edge – devastating as that was to many.

What finally did it for me was a Kansas City Conference involving some of the biggest and most respected prophets in the whole movement. This conference took place less than two weeks after the original Paul Cain announcement – in late October 2004. As I said, our ministry was based in Kansas City at that time, so I was there personally, and all I can say is that my worst fears were confirmed in abundance. This was truly the final straw.

Here is the report that I issued on our International Email List immediately following the Conference:

"I'M LEAVING THE PROPHETIC MOVEMENT"

- Andrew Strom (Nov 3, 2004).

A report on the Kansas City 'Whitedove' Conference, Oct 28-30, 2004. (-Main speakers: Bob Jones, Paul Keith Davis, Bobby Conner, John Paul Jackson, Shawn Bolz – plus Jim Goll and others).

It is with great sadness that I make the following report.

I said last week that the conference in Kansas City this past weekend would be a pivotal one. It certainly was pivotal for me personally. I wish I could say that there was deep repentance - that the preaching was incredibly anointed and the crowd were on their faces crying before God. I wish I could say that, but I can't. In fact, it seemed to me that the opposite was true. The saddest thing of all is that many people probably came away from this conference saying how "wonderful" and "uplifting" it was (-just as they always do). But I have to tell you, I was grieved to the core by it. Many parts of it I would even describe as spiritually "sick".

Some people believe that the fall of Paul Cain into serious sin is some kind of aberration - just one individual's problem. But I am convinced that the fall of Paul Cain (-who was recognized worldwide as the 'father' of this movement) is a symptom of a much wider disease. The whole movement is sick. As I have stated in previous articles, the 'Prophetic' as we know it is really a "fallen" movement - since the early 1990's. But I always held out hope that it would somehow turn around and get back on track again. In fact, I believed that this conference was a heaven-sent opportunity for that to happen.

However, after what I saw this weekend, I no longer believe this is possible. The deception is now too deep. This movement is being "given over to believe a lie" and I want no part of it. I am cutting myself off, because I cannot afford the disease to spread into what we ourselves are doing. Things have now gotten so bad that we have to separate ourselves - and to do so publicly.

As you know, I requested special prayer from you all last week that a true spirit of Repentance might prevail in this conference. The reason I made this request was because God had woken me up at 6 am the previous Friday and given me a strong word about the conference. (God only wakes me up like this quite rarely - perhaps five times a year).

The word He gave me was that this must be a 'repentance' conference - that this was in essence the "last chance" for the Prophetic movement because it had become more and more corrupt - centered around money and 'ear-tickling' words, false prophecy and so-on. This was a gathering of KEY prophets at a moment in time when the 'father' of the movement had just fallen. It was God's ideal moment for a truly "solemn assembly". (And yes -

I did write and pass this word on - in person - to the three main leaders of the conference).

However, what actually eventuated at this event seemed to me to be more akin to a circus than a solemn assembly. The music, the concert-style lighting, the stage dancers, the groaning tables stacked high with books and CD's for sale, the 'ear-tickling', the hype, the $40.00 door fee (plus extra offerings taken each session) - and that's just for starters.

What really bothered me about the weekend was the total lack of any truly 'prophetic' preaching. There was some good stuff on Self-pity and Bitterness right near the start, but after that it was mostly downhill. As always, there were plenty of anecdotes and tales of angelic visitations, etc. There were Scriptures quoted and a few helpful insights. But as far as a message that truly pierces and challenges and convicts - well, don't go looking for that in THIS prophetic movement! In fact, there were warnings AGAINST any message that might come across as even slightly "condemning", and there was even one of those cute talks on the need for "loving oneself", etc.

Today's prophets seem to talk a lot ABOUT the 'sword of the Lord' but never actually bring it to bear. They bring no piercing word. And thus the entire movement is open to great deception. And instead of REPENTANCE, people are getting all kinds of counterfeit spiritual experiences. There seems to be almost no discernment at all.

The ON-STAGE DANCING throughout this conference was a good example. Now, I myself am a rock musician, but from the beginning these dance items had a rather 'wild' aspect to them that truly made me uncomfortable in my spirit. There was even one that came across like a sensual 'Harem' dance. Much of it really felt "off" - and almost anyone who sees the videos will tell you so. Even the worship had a very "tribal" feel to it at times. And by Day Three they were doing dance items with just loud voodoo-style drums only - and leaping around in a frenzied circle making weird cries to the super-amplified beat. The feeling in the room was so *oppressive and "pagan" during this, that I could hardly even bear to stay in there. Then came one of the most shocking statements of the whole conference - from one of the main prophets. He got up and said that people may feel uncomfortable with such obviously "pagan" type dancing, but that it was originally God's type of dancing and we were just now 'stealing back' what the pagans had stolen from God!*

I have to admit, this was the last straw for me. What could be more blatant? What kind of 'spirits' do they think are being transmitted to people who open themselves up to that music? There is no discernment in this movement at all.

Now, I do not primarily blame the dancers. They were young and possibly immature. (-They weren't actually from 'Whitedove' itself). Clearly, most of the blame lies with the main prophets who invited them in and openly endorsed and promoted what was happening the whole time. They would get up and publicly acclaim these dance items, thus ensuring that the spirit of it would pervade the entire event. And indeed it did - more and more.

Remember, most of the major "movers and shakers" of the Prophetic movement were at this conference, going along with this stuff. I repeat what I said earlier: This movement demonstrates absolutely NO DISCERNMENT. I urge everyone to GET OUT NOW, before even worse is brought in. I believe this movement is RIGHT NOW being given over to deception by God - and it is going to get much worse.

Even the 'spiritual' moments in this conference often had strong touches of "Charis-mania" excess about them. And this was not the 'harmless, silly' kind of excess, either. It was at a level where I believe demonic spirits of deception were clearly at work. By the last session the audience was so hyped that they threw away all inhibition and leapt into the 'pagan' dancing themselves with wild abandon. And one of the main prophets even got up and announced that there were angels in the room going around "blowing on peoples' fingers" if only they would lift them up in the air. That particular part sounds silly, but actually the whole thing by this stage had become awful beyond words. Virtually every day I came home utterly grieved and depressed. I had come to this conference with great expectancy and hope, thinking that the return of [the main KC prophet] may bring a renewal of all that was originally good about this movement. I literally came as a 'friend' and they turned me into an enemy in the space of three days.

Below are the SPECIFIC THINGS that God told me He has against this movement as a whole:

-The giving and receiving of "ear-tickling" words.
-The giving and receiving of money in expectation of prophecy.
-False words and false teaching.
-The lack of a true Repentance message.
-The spiritual 'blindness' that allows familiar spirits and spirits of divination to flourish.
-The failure of this movement to judge itself, meaning that God must judge it.
-The idolizing of well-known prophets - placing them on a pedestal.
-And so on....

WHAT NOW FOR US?

Well, obviously, with great sadness we must now totally cut ourselves off from today's Prophetic Movement. Any related links and articles will be removed from our web-site immediately.

As you know, for some time now I have spoken of the 'John-the-Baptist' type ministries that must arise to preach REPENTANCE in the Western nations. -Preachers of righteousness with a piercing word, like the Finneys, the Wesleys and the Whitefields of old. Such ministries are essential for true Revival to come. I now see that this new move must completely "separate itself" from the influence of the existing Prophetic movement. We need a completely 'NEW' Prophetic, and to keep it from being tainted by the sickness that has infected the old, there must be a complete *cutting-off and a "leaving behind".*

I urge all of you to take this before the Lord for yourself. We live in very dangerous times, and I believe the old Prophetic literally stands under the judgment of God...

I would ask that you forward this announcement to as many Lists as you can, and to your Christian friends. We want it as widely known as possible that we have cut off all relations with the current Prophetic movement - and why we did it.

As you can tell, it has been a terribly sad and devastating weekend for myself and my family. We would truly appreciate your prayers at this time, my friends.

God bless you all.

I guess you will not be surprised that I was flooded with literally hundreds upon hundreds of emails after I sent out the above report. In fact, my In-box was crammed from morning until night. The whole thing took on a life of its own and people were 'forwarding' it all over the Internet. Even leaders from Prophetic circles were writing to me. And to my surprise, many responses seemed genuinely supportive of the stand I had taken.

I then put out a follow-up article to highlight other things that needed saying. And the first thing I felt I needed to clarify was that I was not speaking from 'rejection' or hurt or some kind of critical spirit, but rather out of a genuine desire to see these vital issues addressed: *"For many years, even when I was truly disturbed by something I usually avoided "naming names" as much as possible. I do not approve of the 'Heresy Hunters' who seem to take such delight in maligning Spirit-filled ministries across the Internet. There is no delight in such things for me. Only grief and sadness that the name of Jesus is once again being brought down into the mud. We live in very sad times in the church today, don't we?"*

I then went on to address several issues which built on what I had said in my first article:

"...Speaking of the sad and grievous state of this movement, I wonder how many of you received the following notice from the Elijah List recently about a forthcoming 'School of the Prophets': "God is releasing a new level of revelation that goes beyond just operating in the nine gifts of the Spirit.... Sessions will cover topics like Hearing the Voice of God, Activating your Spiritual Senses, Third Heaven Experiences, and Exploring Spirit Realms." The advertised speakers are Todd Bentley, Stacey Campbell, Larry Randolph, Paul Keith Davis, and Bobby Conner.

Now, I have come across Todd Bentley's teachings on "How to visit the Third Heaven" before, and I tell you, it is nothing less than 'Guided Visualization' taken straight out of the New Age movement. Nothing less and nothing more. It is exactly the same. And I want you to know that if you attend these kinds of things, or allow these men to 'guide' you or lay hands upon you, then you are opening yourself up to all kinds of spirits and demonic counterfeits. As I have stated before, this movement has absolutely NO DISCERNMENT at all. It has sunk into such deception that its leaders are opening people up to all kinds of demonic experiences on a daily basis. It has no idea that it is even doing it. -It behaves exactly like a movement that has been "given over to deception" by God. I urge again that everyone reading this would prayerfully consider CUTTING OFF all ties to this movement, lest you yourself become tainted by it.

It is with great sadness that I make the above points. I have refrained from saying such things in the past, but I can no longer do so, because untold people are being spiritually damaged by what is going on. Please understand my heart in this."

Below are further highlights from this second article:

HOW TO AVOID DECEPTION

What a lot of people don't seem to recognize is the sheer level of 'peer pressure' and "crowd manipulation" that is going on at many of these events. They end up being led into doing things they feel uncomfortable with, just because "everybody else" is doing it. They squash down their discernment. They ignore the "little voice" or the tiny 'alarm bells' inside them that are trying to get their attention. And thus, multitudes of Christians are being led astray – and paying through the nose for the privilege. I urge anyone reading this who has ever squashed down their discernment and participated in such things, to get before God and REPENT of opening yourself up in that way. It is very important that you confess this before God and ask His forgiveness. RENOUNCE all deception in Jesus' name.

REDEFINING "PROPHET"

Just because I have cut myself off from today's Prophetic movement does not mean that I believe there is no place for prophets in the church. In fact, I believe we need true prophets now more than ever. But you will notice that there has been a subtle shift in the use of the term "prophet" over the last 25 years, and I believe we need to get back to the original meaning. It was not long ago that when you spoke of a 'prophet' you were usually referring to someone like Keith Green, Leonard Ravenhill or David Wilkerson – someone who was crying out to the lukewarm church, "REPENT." And if you look down the annals of history, you will find that there has never been a true Prophetic movement that did not have this as its core message. Every true Prophetic movement, right from the Old Testament down through every Revival and Awakening that I have ever studied, has been a movement of REPENTANCE. And yet we find today a movement that calls itself "Prophetic" – but with spiritual 'revelations' and words of knowledge at its core. -No piercing word. This is the precise reason why it has gone off the rails. -It has abandoned its age-old message. It's 'word' has been corrupted.

I am convinced that God IS going to raise up true prophets in this hour to cry to the lukewarm church "Repent". There is a movement coming that is utterly different from that which we have seen. God is coming to clean house. The "shaking" has already begun. And the "John-the-Baptists" whom God has prepared in the caves and wildernesses are about to arise and speak His word – just as in every Great Awakening down through history.

Some people asked me if I was going to shut down our web-sites and email Lists. Not at all. The whole point of what we're doing is to call forth and encourage these "John-the-Baptists" whom God is raising up in this hour. We will not stop crying aloud until we see a great 'Repentance' Revival sweeping this nation from coast to coast.

As I said, there were literally thousands of responses to these articles and some of the "big names" even felt forced to respond – but sadly not in a very satisfying way. At no time did I feel that there could be any genuine change in the movement as a result of the stand I had taken.

And sadly, many of the emails that I was receiving from around the world simply confirmed what a disastrous mess the Prophetic had become, and that I was right in cutting myself off from it completely.

Several weeks after my first 'Leaving' article, I shared the following on our email List:

It has not been the emails that disagree with me or accuse me of being "divisive", etc, that bring me to tears. It is the emails from all over the world that strongly AGREE with me and tell me of other horrors that they have witnessed themselves. I sat at my computer last night getting sadder and sadder as I read account after account of the sickness that has spread around the globe as part of this movement. -It is actually WORSE than I ever imagined... We are talking here about a movement where it is encouraged for people to interact with "Orbs of light" that come hovering down (-a major prophetic ministry does this) or to pay money for personal "dream interpretations". We are talking about a movement that teaches people how to "visualize" their way into the 'Third Heaven' and sometimes holds 'Presbytery' days where you can book a half-hour personal appointment with a prophet for a hefty fee. We are talking about a movement that majors on 'manifestations', "portals" and weird 'visitations'. In every way it more closely resembles the New Age movement than anything Christian. In fact, more and more I am seeing that this movement is utterly dominated by a spirit of DIVINATION and fortune-telling. It is sick beyond words. And its prophets are utterly blind. Even now, they rush to hold a huge 'Visitations' gathering in Hollywood... I am close to tears even now, just writing about it. It is so awful what this movement has become. Please STAY AWAY from it, my friends. We are talking about DEMONIC encounters here. "And no marvel; for Satan himself is transformed into an angel of light. Therefore it is no great thing if his ministers also be transformed as the ministers of righteousness" (2 Cor 11:14-15). We truly are in the Last Days.

To the casual reader it may be hard to see how all this relates to modern "revivals" like the one in Lakeland, Florida – but actually it does – very much. Because the same Prophetic movement that brought forth the "orbs of light", the strange 'angel' visitations, the jewels, the "Third Heaven" experiences, etc, is the exact same one that brought forth Todd Bentley and the Healing Revival. (We will see proof of this in the next chapter). That is how I knew so much about Todd's ministry long before he went to Florida. He was part of the same Prophetic movement that I was – but we were at opposite ends of the spectrum. I was a holiness and repentance guy; he was an "angels and gold-dust" guy. And in fact, it was exactly these kinds of bizarre teachings and phenomena (which I had always been against) that ended up forcing me right out of the movement altogether.

Perhaps it is time that we talk a little bit more about these "manifestations" that are found right through the modern Prophetic movement, the Toronto/"River" movement and others. That is what the following chapter is all about.

CHAPTER TWO

WHAT ON EARTH??

Originally the word 'Charismatic' was used to describe people and groups who believed in the Baptism of the Holy Spirit accompanied by biblical gifts such as "speaking in tongues" and healing, etc. Of course, references to these things are found throughout the New Testament, so there is a very strong biblical foundation behind them. In fact, the overall Pentecostal movement, which believes in these gifts, now numbers in the hundreds of millions worldwide. It has been one of the fastest growing Christian movements in the earth now for many decades. And generally it holds to pretty orthodox evangelical views of Scripture and theology.

But in the last 15 years or so, the 'Charismatic' branch of this movement has begun to embrace all kinds of extra-biblical experiences and 'manifestations'. Some of these seem fairly harmless, but others seem downright bizarre and outlandish. As someone who was around before all of this flooded in, I have a particular perspective on a lot of it, and the effect it has had on the entire movement. And even from the beginning, I have to say that I found much of it deeply disturbing – and I got myself into a lot of trouble for saying so. What were we to make of spiritual drunkenness and "laughing revivals", jerking and animal noises, gold dust, feathers and strange 'angel' encounters, etc? (Please don't think this is "fringe" stuff that we are talking about here. In recent years in the Prophetic movement, such things have become more and more the norm rather than the exception. In fact, today you would be hard-pressed to find any big-time Prophetic meetings in which these kinds of things weren't being sought).

Below I have compiled a number of accounts posted by my readers over the years, about meetings or revivals that they personally attended and things that they saw. As I said, please don't think that these things are "unusual". In Prophetic/'River-revival' circles over the last fifteen years or so, these kinds of things have become all too common:

Barbara wrote:

"I got to the meeting early, excited at the prospect of perhaps seeing a true revival, something I know every believer of Jesus Christ longs to see in the church. It is so desperately needed. As I talked with those waiting, everyone encouraged us that our long trip would not be in vain, that we would be greatly blessed. I purchased some booklets in the lobby excited to learn more about what God was doing. Finally, the meeting began with worship. My excitement and enthusiasm quickly vanished. Something seemed very wrong to me. I thought maybe I was expecting too much. The worship was very typical of the modern contemporary worship that I had been accustomed to, most of the songs familiar, but something didn't seem right in the Spirit.. Then the manifestations began. Young girls walking around gesturing as though they were mentally ill. One of the worship leaders, a female, collapsed on the floor during the worship where she remained for a long time. I kept telling myself.. keep an open mind. I kept asking God.. is this you.. if this is you, give me a peace in my spirit. It never came. As the speakers began to share, I became increasingly disturbed. They spoke of the mystical appearance of the river... and how its power swept into the building and changed everything. They went on and on about manifestations, particularly about bizarre behaviors in which they believed they were birthing things through intercession. The pastor's wife spoke and the entire time she was on the platform she jerked uncontrollably as she told stories of phenomena.

Finally, I could stand it no longer. I looked at my family and said, 'Let's get out of here.' They were quick to agree. I left the materials that I had purchased on the church parking lot. I didn't even want to take them in my car...."

Michael wrote:

"Last Sunday (3 days ago), several young people returned.... Three of the young ladies (16 year old range) exhibited "the jerks" and "writhing like a snake" manifestations. Neither one of these girls would have ever acted like this before, and two of them were downright shy! These were manifested in our Sunday evening service and they were not in control of themselves. They sat in their pews looking as though they belonged in a mental institution. Many in the congregation were laughing at what they saw. I confess, I started to laugh also but did my best to hold it in, not deeming the situation that funny.

On Monday morning during the opening exercises at the church school (grades 1-12, A.C.E.), my daughter told me that the normal 15 minute opening exercises lasted over two hours during which the manifestations of the previous mentioned three girls were passed over to many in the school. My wife, after hearing this, became very disturbed and concerned and requested of me that both she and I would attend the opening exercises on Tuesday, ie. yesterday. The school went through their pledges, etc, and then the pastor preached. His sermon dealt with getting more of God, but to get more of God one would have to get all their sins under the blood, deny themselves completely, and make themselves or put themselves in the way of a blessing. He mentioned that a hindrance to the blessings of God would be if the students thought: "What would people think if I started "jerking" or got 'slain in the spirit'". This was quite emphasized even though all the while the pastor would inject that "this isn't about manifestations". He also emphasized how the children would be playing a big part in the revival that was to start in our church. Well, the sermon ended and then the music started and the altar call began with one student after another going up to the altar. One thing that was very disturbing is that only one song was played, a 30 second piece that goes "Anointing, fall on me, anointing fall on me, let the power of the Holy Ghost fall on me, anointing fall on me." Remember that the altar call lasted at least one hour with this song being played over and over just like a MANTRA!

The manifestations began again, beginning with the girls I previously described and then passing from them over to other children. Several began to jerk, especially the girls. Why the girls? The children just went from one to another laying hands on one another. Beyond what I witnessed on Sunday evening, the following manifestations were seen: Uncontrollable weeping, staggering, unable to stand, stuck to the floor, writhing like a serpent, crawling on hands and knees, mooing, exhaustion. These manifestations are given as manifestations among those involved with Kundalini/Shakti on a chart that I have in front of me. After at least an hour of this, the children went back to their pews, but not until the music had stopped of course, and they just sat there, quiet, not saying a word for at least another 1/2 hour. One of the original three girls stood up and said this was a sovereign work of God, crying all the time. One of the school teachers said that it was good for the kids to be resting now, that it was good to rest after having been in the presence of the Lord. My daughters are not in school today and they won't be in school any more until this thing is settled. This is crazy. I've experienced God's power, I've experienced being baptized with the Holy Ghost, but never in my life did such experiences leave me exhausted or in a state of bewilderment like these young people seemed to be in...."

Philippe wrote:

"I was invited by a friend to visit a church of a great pastor with a powerful healing ministry. I had a dream the night before I went. In that dream I was fighting a big snake with a sort of big knife. During the fight the blood of the snake fell upon the middle of my head. At the time I could not understand, even though I knew Lev

17:11, Gen 9:4, Lev 17:14, "For the SOUL of the flesh is in the BLOOD." I could not believe that the spirit of the serpent could dwell inside of me, because I was and I am still a Christian. Jesus Christ gave me victory over my sins, changed completely my life and set me free. I am very grateful for calvary, I would never willingly forsake the prince of peace for the powers of darkness.

As planned I went to the church, I could not get inside the church because it was already filled with people. I attended the service at the overflow room, also crowded, where there were a big screen TV and some good loud speakers. In the middle of the service, while this great orchestra with the choir and the assembly of God people were singing worship songs, the pastor asked everybody to stand up and to lift up our hands. Couple minutes after I did so, my hands started to shake and very soon all my body was trembling vigorously. The best way to describe it is, I was like a tree "shaken of a mighty wind". Inside the church many sick people testified that they were healed, and hundreds felt the manifestation of the spirit. In spite of the dream I was very glad. I said to myself, I have received the Holy Spirit, even though I knew what Jesus Christ said in Matt 24: 24-25 "For false Christs and false prophets shall rise, and shall shew SIGNS and WONDERS, to SEDUCE, if it were possible, even the elect." Yet I could not believe that the spirit of the serpent could dwell in me that easily because I did not invite him. Gen 3:1 "Now the serpent was more subtil than any beast of the fields which the Lord God had made."

So since then I had a spirit inside of me, any time I started to pray, in a matter of seconds the spirit would come, taking control little by little over my body. The manifestations were so strong, that I think even if I was entirely crippled, at those moments the spirit could make me move and walk, because my body was doing with astonishing strength motions that I did not do, and that I could not do at that surprising speed. I went back to this church of this TV Evangelist four other times. Only once the spirit did not fall upon me. I went to two other churches where the manifestations were also strong. One preacher was so powerful, he does not touch people, he only says something and they fell down and lay on the floor. One could easily count on the fingers the number of worshipers who were not "slain in the spirit". On the floor some were doing the "holy laughter", some were making strange noises, some were shaking and others were lying down frozen like dead. The spirit in me was making me gently dance with the songs, but from time to time it was so strong that I was thrown back violently to my seat, with my head leaning in the back. If the seat was not behind me I wonder what would happen to me. I went three times to see the manifestations and every time the spirit was very strong on me.

One day, while I was at home playing a worship CD of the first church's orchestra the spirit fell once more upon me. I played more songs from other Christian artists. The spirit was enjoying them, and was making me dance slowly. An idea came to my mind, I decided then to test the spirit. 1 John 4:1 - "Beloved, believe not every spirit, but try the spirits whether they are of God: because many false prophets are gone into the world." While I was on my knees, at the end of a song I swiftly changed the CD, and played a non-Christian song, a popular dancing song, a fast rhythm. The spirit was very glad, and was making me dance in a very sexy manner, with my hips. Now no more doubts, I clearly realized that it was the spirit of the Anti-Christ spoken of in 2 Thess 2: 9-12: "Even him, whose coming is after the working of satan with all POWER and SIGNS and lying WONDERS, and all deceivableness in them that perish; because they received not the love of the truth, that they might be saved. And for this cause God shall send them strong delusion, that they should believe a lie: That they all might be damned who believe not the truth, but had pleasure in unrighteousness." Matt 24: 11 - "And many false prophets shall rise, and shall deceive many."

Knowing that I had received an evil spirit in a church was one thing, getting rid of that spirit or spirits was another thing. How could I ask Christians to pray to set me free of a spirit that they believe to be the Holy One? So there I was alone against those demonic powers, with the knowledge that many churches have already been defeated. Even then my hope was in Christ, I did not panic. I was sure He would not forsake me. So I did what He said should be done in those cases. I fasted and I prayed, for three days and three nights I was drinking only water. On the third night, I was too tired to sleep well, but I had a very short dream. I saw two huge hands up in heaven, and the right one was pointing the finger downward at me. I could not understand until I read Luke 11:20: "But if I with the finger of God cast out devils, no doubt the kingdom of God is come upon you." Since then the manifestations of the spirit or spirits ceased, by the grace of God...."

'BB' wrote:

"My husband and I were invited by friends to a meeting. As we were not familiar with him, and he was touted as having a powerful ministry, raising the dead, etc., we went along. I'm still reeling from the shock! What took place was a mockery of God and His holiness. The worship music was OK until the two women on the worship team began to sing "in the spirit" (I sensed it wasn't the Holy Spirit). The words they sang were about God, but the tone was dark, and there just seemed to be something wrong there; it was almost like they were in a trance. Right after that, people started falling down and shrieking, cackling, howling, jerking, etc. It sounded more like the pit of hell than a worship service. He started waving his arm around at people, and they would fall "under the spirit," and he would point his Bible at people and make a whooshing sound like he was zapping them, and they would fall "under the spirit." (Notice I used a small "s"; it wasn't a holy spirit.) I couldn't take any more and I left before he started preaching, but my husband stayed because he wanted to know just where this guy was coming from in his teaching. My husband was grieved to discover that the man said nothing about repentance from sin or living a life of holiness before God. All [he] talked about was love, joy, happiness, relationship with God without any commitment on our part. Not one word about sin or forgiveness for our sin. He claims to have raised 83 people from the dead. How can this be? Is this a case of, "Lord, Lord, we have healed the sick,

cast out demons, raised the dead in your name. And He replied, 'Depart from me; I never knew you?'" What has happened to the churches? They are either dead or crazy! Is there no place that is alive with the pure holiness of God? Are we being judgmental? We are Pentecostal, but we realize that not everything that is spiritual is of God. We want the pure, holy presence of God."

'PW' wrote:

"We attended a service on Saturday evening that was the FALSE Revival. We were told to come down front and join a circle and scream out for the GOD OF ELISHA. Once that happened a bunch of strange manifestations happened and we were told to wait on God because He was going to say something to us. My husband, friend, and I almost had not come to this meeting, but since our other friends had taken our two older daughters to the meeting we sensed we needed to be there to protect them... good thing. As the three of us were in the circle we stuck out like SORE thumbs!! We were commanded to give thanks to God for what He was doing. None of us sensed the Spirit of God in this at all... we were deeply grieved. We were even told to not worry about what was going on because it's in the Book. They did some kind of "wave" thing, but I just closed my eyes and prayed and felt NOTHING but deep sickness for what was happening. Even when they did the shouting thing my lips were pursed together... I don't think I could have uttered a word even if I had wanted to (which I didn't).

To go back, when we first arrived in the sanctuary I was hit with the spirit of drunkenness and I said, God, if this is not of you (we are always being told that this carousing, sensual love for God, drunkenness, and revelry is of Him) then I rebuke it in Jesus' name, and instantly the effects of that spirit left me. That answered that question I had. Towards the end of the pagan circle ritual (that's what it felt like to me) I was led to go kneel at my seat and pray. It became very clear that the days of "blending" in the crowd ARE OVER!

Some of the questions we had and were exploring in the Word were: what does it look like to be filled with the Spirit (does it look like you are drunk)? If we put a scene where pagans were worshipping and dubbed a worship song over it would the people there be able to discern the difference? Is what we are seeing just pagan revelry? We are watchmen on a wall testing the spirits and we do look rather odd as we are not experiencing everything that everyone else is. Is singing the same song for 40 minutes just pagan prayer full of repetition? We have a lot of these questions stirring in us as we are testing the spirits until we can hold on to that which is good.

As we searched the scriptures we found a lot of answers that confirmed what the Spirit was showing us... We all felt extremely cared for by our loving Father that as we have fervently been praying that we would NOT be deceived... HE HAS BEEN FAITHFUL TO GUIDE AND DIRECT OUR STEPS!

At this church we have been attending since January, there is God's Spirit working there on the one hand and demonic spirits on the other and the two are so mixed that at times it is VERY difficult to discern what is what. We have met with the leaders of this church and like them and think they have precious hearts, but they are being deluded. My husband and I already mentioned a huge list of our concerns... the "palm reading" – being called down in front and being made a spectacle of... the jerking... sensual dancing... drunkenness actions... a whole bunch of stuff and they seemed very receptive and even addressed some of those things. We have been wondering if God wants us to RUN for our lives yet or not. The past two services have been outright bizarre and TONS OF HYPE and EMOTIONALISM!

One of the phrases used by a worship leader was: "I was invited to go partying, but didn't go, but when they party they lose their inhibitions and are just who they are and are free, and how much more like that should we be than those in the world." Scary words indeed! They are having this conference in September and showed a video clip of this person leading worship and it just looked like pagan revelry... they are bringing this poison into our town... God deliver us."

'MS' wrote:

"I read your article, "Why I left the Prophetic Movement," and it was so similar to an experience and a reaction that I had at a recent "Prophetic" conference last year. Every observation you had is exactly what I observed! These so-called prophets and worship leaders were ushering in lude and familiar spirits, worshipping angels and opening and going through ungodly spiritual portals. I have never been so grieved and disturbed by anything in my life! And nobody else seemed to notice or care other than my fellow peers/disciples who discerned this also! I was so upset I strongly considered confronting... [the big-name leaders]...

The disturbing thing is that other respectable leaders were not able to discern and bring to correction what was going on. The weirdest part about everything is that one of the spirits that was causing some creepy laughter at the conference followed us to the mall after we left the conference and caused a girl working one of the little booths that sells stuff in the middle of the mall to manifest when we walked by and laugh the same exact way. God showed me that the only reason some of the other leaders could not discern this is that they accepted money and thus the spirit of mammon had blinded their eyes to see what was going on. I wish our fellow Evangelists, Prophets, and Missionaries weren't subjected to being beggars and prostituting their gifts the way the modern church system has forced them to do, making them chase opportunities rather than callings. It's sad."

NOTE: Please pay close attention to the following account, because it is from a woman that I know well to be a very dedicated Spirit-filled Christian – a woman of prayer. And this one directly involves the teachings of Todd Bentley, who later went on to start the Florida Healing revival:

Lynn wrote:

"After receiving the Baptism of the Holy Spirit, God began to do a miracle in my heart and I for the first time in my life understood what real sin was and that it separated you from a Holy God. - What does darkness have to do with light - I began to hate sin - and only wanted to serve God in holiness and with all my heart. He also imparted in me a heart for the Lost - along with a dream of a small vision of hell. My love for the Lord began to grow in leaps and bounds and I would think of Him all the time, as I still do even to this very day. I wanted so much more of him - I was so spiritually hungry for Him. My problem was I began to look for Him in all the wrong places.

My first encounter was to sit under the teachings of Jill Austin - and to be taught and prayed over by her and listen to all her angelic visitations. This just opened up more doors to deception and darkness. It is by the grace of God that I was able to come out of this deception - but not right away and without God radically showing me the error in my ways.

I became introduced to the Prophetic Movement because Jill Austin was with the whole Kansas City prophetic movement and I trusted in her judgment - after all she was a Prophetic voice? I started running around to all the big name conferences - even a prayer person in a few - not realizing that I was operating in the flesh and seeing man more than God. There is a huge deception there that satan makes you think you are chasing after God. I have heard all the stories of angels - angel dust - feathers - not realizing that this was just another deception from satan to distract your worship away from God and to put it on experiences - man and angels - however I did never worship angels - but my focus was on the "Man of God" and how spiritual the Man of God is - and I am telling you, that is exactly what these big-name people live for - they are not millions of dollars rich because they preach the cross and repentance.

There are spirits of darkness that follow most of these big conferences and the Holy Spirit would bring up red flags and allowed me to see this spirit of darkness in two of these big lady conference leaders - even to the point they were screeching - and so I said, Thank you Lord that you have shown me these are false prophets. And so I go looking for the ones who are real - "right!" - still not heeding the small voice of the Holy Spirit within me. - Rodney Howard Brown - and the Holy Spirit still showed me the darkness and spirit he operated in - so I decide to check out Patricia King and Todd Bentley and, ignorant of their third heaven guided visualizations, attended a five day conference of Patricia King and then two of Todd Bentley's conferences and began to imagine third heaven visitations - guided visualization - still not realizing that these are actually spirits of darkness - the New Age calls them spirit guides - demons is what they are. And so I bought Todd Bentley's teaching on third heaven visitations and brought it home to listen to.

I was in my living room laying on the floor listening to the teaching on how to visualize the third heaven and what to say and was getting caught up into his teaching and all of a sudden I began to shake uncontrollably and jerk and groan, and no sooner had this taken place I became frozen stiff - I could not move any part of my body and I knew this was a demon trying to take hold of me, and so with all the effort I could muster I cried out, "God save me - Jesus help me" - and as soon as I cried out to the Lord my body went limp. God spared me that night and I will be forever grateful.

I spent much of the night in tears asking God to forgive me - and renouncing all the hands laid on me and all the awful deception I had opened myself up to, and most of all grieving the Holy Spirit within me and setting a horrible example of the true Power and person of the Holy Spirit

So it is very hard for me to be quiet and not sound the alarm when these things come up, for I have been there, done that - several years back - and I will warn and sound the alarm and tell people

- 28 -

that many of these walk in spiritual darkness - oh, they bring enough truth to make it seem they are the called true apostles/prophets of God! May many be spared from their deception..."

ROOTS OF THE HEALING REVIVAL

Please note that in the last account by Lynn, she was introduced to these visualization techniques (identical to the New Age) through the teachings of Todd Bentley. Was this a departure for Todd – a rare mis-step? No, not at all. As stated earlier, Todd is well known in Prophetic circles for being at the forefront of almost every strange fad that has swept through that movement. His mentors in these things have been people like Patricia King (from 'Extreme Prophetic') and Bob Jones (ex-Kansas city prophet) – both big names in Prophetic circles. Todd Bentley has been into this stuff for years. In fact, in many ways it dominates his ministry.

As stated earlier, the above experiences are quite typical of today's "Prophetic/Toronto/River-Revival" meetings, where all discernment seems to have gone out the window and seemingly anything goes – including spiritual drunkenness, jerking, hysterical laughter, animal sounds, stomach cramps, soaking, birthing, "third heaven portals", gold dust, feathers, jewels, seeing angels or orbs of light, and every other kind of spiritual manifestation that you can imagine. All of this in an atmosphere that often seems the very opposite of the majestic Lord of glory described in Scripture as "holy, holy, holy." In fact, it couldn't be further away if it tried. (Please note that the average Pentecostal meeting is certainly not like this. And not every Prophetic meeting either. But generally it is the Prophetic/Toronto/River circles where you will find this stuff today - hugely popular as they are).

Sadly, when this "manifestations mania" first came flooding in around 1994/95, there were very few Charismatic leaders who stood up against it. I remember Art Katz writing one article against it, Derek Prince issuing several warnings, as well as lesser-knowns such as England's Clifford Hill and a few others. I myself became quite unpopular with many of my prophetic colleagues by publishing strong warnings about it from about 1995 onwards. But largely the whole crazy mess flooded in almost unopposed. And immediately it took over. Discernment was largely gone. Common sense went with it. And in my view, what truth and light was left in the Prophetic movement was overrun and almost completely obliterated within months. A deep sickness had invaded the camp. And this of course is what sowed the seeds for my own total renunciation of the Prophetic movement some years later. And sadly it is also where we find the roots of the current Healing revival.

In the mid-1990s, it had been Rodney Howard Browne and the Toronto Blessing that were the biggest carriers of this "anointing". In those early days it was mostly about spiritual drunkenness, hysterical laughter, jerking and animal noises. Then came the Brownsville, Pensacola and Sunderland revivals – which certainly imparted this same anointing – yet had quite a different flavor to them. But after all these movements began to die down, it was largely up to the Prophetic movement to keep the flame alive – and to keep adding new and more extreme experiences - lest people get "bored" with the same old stuff.

Thus we find in the late 1990s and early 2000s the arrival of 'gold dust', jewels, feathers, oil, visualization, "portals" and strange 'angel' encounters. From my days in the Prophetic movement, I can say that Todd Bentley was definitely at the forefront of a lot this stuff, along with several of his colleagues. Which leads us directly to the current Healing revival.

Briefly, for those who are unaware, the Florida Healing revival began when Todd Bentley held a series of meetings at Stephen Strader's Ignite Church in Lakeland Florida in April 2008. Healings began to occur and the meetings were extended. Then God TV began to broadcast the meetings and Charisma magazine and other media began to promote what was happening. People began to come from all over the world to attend. Leaders were specifically targeted by Todd Bentley to receive an "impartation" of his anointing, so they could take it back with them when they left. Before long the crowds were so large that they had to move into an 8000-seat arena. And soon there was talk of "stadiums". It didn't take long before the influence of this anointing was spreading around the world, much as the Toronto Blessing had fourteen years before.

TODD BENTLEY & HIS ANGELS

We have already seen the terrible spiritual danger of Todd Bentley's "Guided Visualization" techniques for visiting the 'Third Heaven'.

But he had been into this kind of thing for ages. In fact, when I was involved with the Prophetic movement, I always regarded Todd as one of the most extreme of all – because he had no qualms about promoting female angels, wealth-getting angels and every kind of dubious experience or 'anointing' you can imagine. And there was real "power" behind it. That is what alarmed me. It wasn't just hype. People were having real 'power encounters' with this stuff.

Let me give you some examples – from Todd's own writings – of how he would lead people into encounters with these 'angels'. The following extracts are from Todd's 2003 article 'Angelic Hosts':

"So when I need a financial breakthrough I don't just pray and ask God for my financial breakthrough. I go into intercession and become a partner with the angels by petitioning the Father for the angels that are assigned to getting me money: "Father, give me the angels in heaven right now that are assigned to get me money and wealth. And let those angels be released on my behalf. Let them go into the four corners of the earth and gather me money..."
[Editor's Note: If you have been around real witchcraft, you will notice that they send out their "spirits" in exactly the same way to get them money as well. Very dangerous – and totally unscriptural].

Todd Bentley continues:

"EMMA, ANGEL OF THE PROPHETIC

"Now let me talk about an angelic experience with Emma. Twice Bob Jones asked me about this angel that was in Kansas City in 1980: "Todd, have you ever seen the angel by the name of Emma?" He asked me as if he expected that this angel was appearing to me. Surprised, I said, "Bob, who is Emma?" He told me that Emma was the angel that helped birth and start the whole prophetic movement in Kansas City in the 1980s. She was a mothering-type angel that helped nurture the prophetic as it broke out. Within a few weeks of Bob asking me about Emma, I was in a service in Beulah, North Dakota.

"In the middle of the service I was in conversation with Ivan and another person when in walks Emma. As I stared at the angel with open eyes, the Lord said, "Here's Emma." I'm not kidding. She floated a couple of inches off the floor. It was almost like Kathryn Khulman in those old videos when she wore a white dress and looked like she was gliding across the platform. Emma appeared beautiful and young - about 22 years old - but she was old at the same time. She seemed to carry the wisdom, virtue and grace of Proverbs 31 on her life. She glided into the room, emitting brilliant light and colors. Emma carried these bags and began pulling gold out of them. Then, as she walked up and down the aisles of the church, she began putting gold dust on people... Within three weeks of that visitation, the church had given me the biggest offering I had ever received to that point in my ministry. Thousands of dollars! Thousands!... During this visitation the pastor's wife (it was an AOG church) got totally whacked by the Holy Ghost - she began running around barking like a dog or squawking like a chicken as a powerful prophetic spirit came on her. Also, as this prophetic anointing came on her, she started getting phone numbers of complete strangers and calling them up on the telephone and prophesying over them... Then angels started showing up in the church." (From 'Angelic Hosts' by Todd Bentley).

Doesn't it sound like there might be a possibility of 'false' angels here – of counterfeit spirits masquerading as "angels of light"? Isn't it possible that alien spirits could be the source of some of this 'power'? The Bible explicitly commands us: "Do not believe every spirit, but test the spirits, whether they are of God; because many false prophets have gone out into the world" (1 John 4:1). But it doesn't sound to me as if much "testing the spirits" is going on in some of these encounters.

Now I have nothing personal against Todd whatsoever. I don't even know him on a personal level – so this has nothing to do with that. But his ministry has always greatly concerned me – because of this bizarre "power" attached to it – like we see in the above account. This is nothing unusual for him at all – contacting these 'angels' and putting his audience in touch with them. His meetings have often been full of this kind of thing. But sadly I have to say that to me it has always seemed more akin to the 'Kundalini' manifestations of the New Age than anything Christian – and I have to seriously wonder what spirit is behind it all. And now here he is, leading a worldwide movement that involves spreading his 'anointing' around the globe.

More recently, Todd stated that in one of his "Third Heaven" trips he literally visited the small cabin where the apostle Paul lives in Heaven. Paul apparently told him that the authorship of the book of Hebrews was unclear because he wrote it with the personal help of Abraham the Patriarch: *"Paul said, "When I was in the third heaven, Abraham was with me like you are with me now. Abraham himself shared (information) with me and I simply wrote it" (in the Book of Hebrews). "The authorship isn't clear because it was Abraham and I; Abraham shared the content with me."* Todd's 'Third Heaven' tales are full of such astonishing claims - and of course, more angels. (See 'A Face To Face Encounter' – Part 2 - by Todd Bentley).

Some people think that I actually "enjoy" bringing up these kinds of things. But the fact is that I am deeply grieved by every bit of it. In fact I truly detest having to talk about this stuff at all. But what happens if something is seriously amiss in such an influential movement and yet no warnings are given? Is it right to be silent in such a case? What about the precious sheep? Shouldn't they be warned?

Lest anyone think that Todd may have changed his ways in recent times, you should know that he is constantly mentioning his 'angels' in the current Florida meetings also.

In one recent video from Florida that anyone can watch on the Internet, Todd speaks of the angel that is going to "visit the children" and then he begins to jerk and laugh uncontrollably more and more. He prays that a 'drunken glory' will move across the whole place – and you can see it happen in the audience. In another video he has German preacher Stefan Driess on stage with him and they both weave drunkenly as Stefan describes the angel encounter that he just had. Todd then imparts his 'anointing' to Stefan by kneeing him in the stomach and Stefan falls to the ground, jerking uncontrollably. These bizarre manifestations and the 'angels' that accompany them seem to be all through the Florida revival. In fact angels are being given credit for many of the healings there. (Please watch the change in Todd's EYES during a lot of these manifestations also. Frightening!) One eyewitness described the "impartation" lines in Florida this way: *"As far (and I mean as far) as I could see, masses of people on the floor shaking, shivering, dazed looking, completely out or unconscious looking."*

As I have said, this is all the same kind of stuff that Todd has been involved in for a very long time. There is very little "new" in it. In fact, you could say that a lot of it is almost 'Toronto' to a tee. But this time both Todd and Bob Jones credit an angel that carries the "Winds of Change" for this new revival in Florida – an angel that they say is still driving it. As one young preacher commented who has been following the Florida meetings closely, Todd seems to talk about his "healing angel" even more than he talks about Jesus. Yes - exactly!

As noted earlier, we are warned explicitly in Scripture that the devil "transforms himself into an angel of light" (2 Cor 11:14). We are also warned about those who "worship angels" (Col 2:18), and that any man or angel bringing a false gospel should be "accursed" (Gal 1:8). Are there true angels from God that sometimes appear to people? Yes – certainly! And they bring with them the awesome holy fear of the Lord. But the Bible also warns us again and again of the false. In fact, we are told repeatedly that in the Last Days will come false prophets with "signs and wonders to deceive, if possible, even the elect" (Mark 13:22). So do we really believe that the devil is unable to perform miracles? Have we forgotten what the Bible clearly says?

When Scripture specifically warns us that in the End Times will come 'seducing spirits', doctrines of demons and "lying signs and wonders", are we actually going to listen – or ignore it? Shouldn't we be more alert for these things now than at any other time in history?

Some make the point that Todd obviously had a strong healing gift right from the start of his ministry – so some of the healings in Florida may be genuinely from God. Yes – I agree that this is possible – even likely. But how can we trust anything at all coming from this source if it has become so tainted with all this pollution? Do we want such a man laying hands on us and imparting "anointings" or spirits into us? Are the 'angels' behind Todd's ministry really from God at all?

MOST "CONTAGIOUS" ANOINTING

Todd Bentley has declared that his Florida anointing is the most "contagious" that he has ever imparted to people. (In other words, the most easily transferable). And indeed this seems to be the case. It is spreading rapidly throughout the world.

As one missionary wrote after watching the Florida meetings: *"Todd Bentley constantly manifests his "anointing" by shaking his head back and forth, and by his body physically shaking. These manifestations also happen frequently in those who he imparts to. He will even wave his arms over the audience, shouting, "Fire! Fire! Fire!" and then people in the audience will start manifesting. Some appear to be convulsing, and some even as if they are being thrashed by a spirit."*

In a CBN News interview, Todd stated: *"Our focus here in Florida every night is I lay hands on every single person who comes - whether it's 5,000, 10,000 - And I'm praying every night, 'God, give it away, give it away, give it away.' And that's the focus here: Impartation."*

And indeed there are more and more reports of this anointing being transmitted from Florida to other states and nations across the globe. And what happens when it enters these other settings?

A report from England tells of a preacher who brought Todd's anointing back from Florida and now has it manifesting in his UK meetings: *"Fire, a burning sensation, was felt all over people's bodies... There were outbursts of joy, drunkenness and spontaneous healings throughout the meeting."* Another eyewitness from Hawaii reports the arrival of the 'Florida anointing' there: *"As the Pastor laid hands on the people he yelled with great force, "FIRE!!!" Folks dropped like flies. People were all over the floor... howling, crying and sobbing in anguish, laughing, shaking, some convulsing under the power, and falling as if some thunder fell on their heads."*

A man from Clearwater, Florida says that a number of people from his fellowship have attended the revival and then brought the 'anointing' back with them. Here is what he personally observed:

"These are the effects that I have witnessed on people who have attended this movement and either have had hands laid on them or claim to have been imparted with "the spirit":
-They come back with this kind of childlike drunken stupor.
-Descriptions of a burning sensation either in their veins, heads or

stomachs.
-Descriptions of being washed back and forth like the waves in the ocean;
-Dancing about like drunk...
-Inappropriate yelling and screaming like they're at a football game;
-Young men whistling over and over and holding their heads and claiming that they "feel the Holy Spirit about to split them in two";
-One young man's back two teeth turned completely to some metallic finish.
-People with their eyes rolled in the back of their heads and weaving around like they're lost.
-Women just gyrating and pulsating like they're being ravaged from behind from some unseen force.
-Drunken uncontrollable laughter in the middle of a solemn prayer time...
-People being "slain in the spirit"... just falling down and being unable to move (like something's holding them down).

These things above are things that I've witnessed in people attending the congregation I do. Sadly, many are friends."

Another eyewitness from the USA writes:

A friend of mine invited me to a church where the ministry team brought back a "Fire" from the Lakeland revival... First, there was praise and worship. The pastor's wife was moderating, but she could not complete her sentences because she was 'drunk in the Spirit.' She imitated the type of sounds I read in your blog. I saw people breaking out into uncontrollable laughter. I came with my Bible to receive a word... There was no teaching or preaching. Just testimonies. They talked about their experience in Lakeland, how the attendance grew to over 10k. Where was the word? I did not find any. I also heard a sound BAM and then I saw someone being slain in the spirit. I was not going to do what other people did. Although I was hesitant (probably the Holy Spirit telling me to RUN from this mess), yet I did come up to the line for impartation of this fire. I felt the leadership team was disappointed I didn't fall to the floor or break out in laughter. I did feel a sensation in my hands like fire. I pondered on what happened over the weekend.

Today I looked up Lakeland and read your blog. I should have kept with my original thought and stayed out of that prayer line. I repented immediately..."

Another man from the U.S. Northeast reports:

I went to West Haven, CT, last weekend. It was supposed to be a group of ministries getting together to encourage one another and pray. Some of them had been to Lakeland and were jerking and yelling "Oh-wooooooowwww" and then they began to talk about how Bob Jones called it the 3rd wave... They all were in what they call Drunken Glory...

That church in CT last night started having their own revival services and impartation, and it has broken out down there... The Northeast is really the place that is becoming the hotbed of this. They are having services all over for impartation and daily reports are breaking out about it. I am being told that I am deceived for questioning it. They are telling me that I am going against the Holy Spirit...

Many reports from the USA now speak of pastors having hands laid on them to receive the "Florida anointing" – so they can pass it on to their own congregations.

CHARISMA DARES TO QUESTION

Interestingly, several weeks after Charisma Magazine published a glowing report in April 2008 basically promoting everything that was happening in Florida, their Editor J. Lee Grady put out a piece that was quite different in tone. It was entitled, 'Honest Questions About the Lakeland Revival'... *"I support any holy outbreak of revival fervor. But let's be careful to guard ourselves from pride and error."*

While Mr. Grady was careful to state that he supported what was happening in Lakeland and believed in the healings, he then went on to bring some very serious warnings, which truly raised questions about his previous remarks:

"I fear another message is also being preached subtly in Lakeland—a message that cult-watchers would describe as a spiritual counterfeit. Bentley is one of several charismatic ministers who have emphasized angels in the last several years. He has taught about angels who bring financial breakthroughs or revelations, and he sometimes refers to an angel named Emma who supposedly played a role in initiating a prophetic movement in Kansas City in the 1980s. Bentley describes Emma as a woman in a flowing white dress who floats a few feet off the floor... Paul was adamant that preoccupation with angels can lead to serious deception.

"We need to tread carefully here! We have no business teaching God's people to commune with angels or to seek revelations from them. And if any revival movement—no matter how exciting or passionate—mixes the gospel of Jesus with this strange fire, the results could be devastating. We need to remember that Mormonism was born out of one man's encounter with a dark angel who claimed to speak for God."

But the Charisma Editor did not leave his warnings there. He went on to caution about 'bizarre manifestations' also:

"In many recent charismatic revivals, ministers have allowed people to behave like epileptics on stage—and they have attributed their attention-getting antics to the Holy Spirit. We may think it's all in fun (you know, we're just "acting crazy" for God) but we should be more concerned that such behavior feeds carnality and grieves the Spirit.

"When exotic manifestations are encouraged, people can actually get a religious high from jerking, vibrating, screaming or acting intoxicated. (I have even been around people who writhed as if in pain, or made sexual noises—thinking this was a legitimate spiritual experience.)... When we put bizarre behavior on the platform we imply that it is normative. Thus more strange fire is allowed to spread."

Amazingly, Mr. Grady did not even stop there. He had a third caution to bring:

"Beware of hype and exaggeration... Some of the language used during the Lakeland Revival has created an almost sideshow atmosphere. People are invited to "Come and get some." Miracles are supposedly "popping like popcorn." Organizers tout it as the greatest revival in history..."

I, for one, certainly appreciated J. Lee Grady's courage in putting out such warnings. Of course it didn't mean that he had truly "changed sides". There was still a lot of equivocating going on. But I had to admire the fact that the Editor of Charisma would dare to publish such clear-cut warnings. And please note that he highlighted the exact same pitfalls and deceptions that we have been discussing in this book. In fact, we can find a lot of "confirmation" in Mr. Grady's comments – that there is indeed something seriously amiss at the heart of the Florida movement.

A "KUNDALINI" AWAKENING?

One of the things that has been pointed out for years about the manifestations found in these movements is their incredible similarity with the 'Kundalini'/ Shakti manifestations found in Hinduism and other Eastern religions. I guess this is a difficult thing to accept – because it seems so incredible to many. How could such a spirit find its way into the Christian church? But the similarities are indeed remarkable. Is it possible that an "alien" spirit somehow invaded the church in the early 1990s – and then continued to mutate and adapt to the church environment? What would such a spirit look like in a Christian setting?

If you search for Kundalini and Shakti on the Internet, you will find that multitudes of people in the New Age and Eastern religions still experience these powerful manifestations. Often this is with the help of a Guru, who touches them on the forehead (this is called 'Shaktipat') – so that these people can experience a "Kundalini Awakening".

As researcher Robert Walker wrote in 1995:

"Few Christians realise that for thousands of years gurus have operated with gifts of healing, miracles, gifts of knowledge, and intense displays of spiritual consciousness as they stretch out and connect with a cosmic power which, though demonic in origin, is very real. The meetings which mystic Hindu gurus hold are called 'Darshan'. At these meetings devotees go forward to receive spiritual experience from a touch by the open palm of the hand, often to the forehead, by the guru in what is known as the Shakti Pat or divine touch. The raising of the spiritual experience is called raising Kundalini... After a period when the devotee has reached a certain spiritual elevation they begin to shake, jerk, or hop or squirm uncontrollably, sometimes breaking into uncontrolled animal noises or laughter as they reach an ecstatic high. These manifestations are called 'Kriyas'. Devotees sometimes roar like lions and show all kinds of physical signs during this period. Often devotees move on to higher states of spiritual consciousness and become inert physically and appear to slip into an unconsciousness when they lose sense of what is happening around them. This state is called 'samadhi' and it leads to a deeper spiritual experience."

As the guru Shri Yogānandji Mahārāja wrote:

"When Your body begins trembling, hair stands on roots, you laugh or begin to weep without your wishing, your tongue begins

to utter deformed sounds, you are filled with fear or see frightening visions... the Kundalini Shakti has become active."

In China there is a popular Kundalini-type movement called 'Qigong'. When Yan Xin, a Chinese Qigong spiritual Master, gave a talk to a crowd in San Francisco in 1991, the San Francisco Chronicle reported that many in the crowd began to experience what Yan called "spontaneous movements". He told his audience, "Those who are sensitive might start having some strong physical sensations – or start laughing or crying. Don't worry. This is quite normal."

Now doesn't a lot of this sound awfully familiar? Isn't it virtually identical to what we have seen in the church over the last 15 years or so? An empowered leader touching people on the head and all these weird manifestations occurring? Could it be the same spirit?

One thing we need to take note of is that such manifestations are found NOWHERE in the Bible. The Scripture does describe miracles and healings and gifts of the Spirit. But these things are very different. Even in the Charismatic movement all this is relatively "new". It only started to flood in around 1994. So where did it come from? The Holy Spirit, or another spirit altogether?

Please compare the below account from a modern 'revival' with the 'Kundalini' manifestations above. One of my readers sent this to me some years ago – but it is very typical of what many have experienced:

"I inadvertently got prayed over by some people who had received "The Toronto Blessing". I ended up that night with uncontrollable flopping and shaking of my limbs, being drunk in spirit and uncontrollable laughter. At the time it felt right. But later as time went on, these manifestations came at inopportune times and were uncontrollable. My arms and legs would shake when trying to pray for people or when just sitting in church. My legs would give out and I would have to catch my balance just to stand upright while worshipping. It soon became clear to me that this was not the Holy

Spirit and so I repented of allowing myself to receive this spirit and asked God to take it away from me. Praise Him, He did!"

Now there is no doubt that a Hindu Guru would describe the above as a 'Kundalini Awakening'. It is virtually identical in every respect. And yet we in the church called it a Blessing from God! And seemingly this same anointing continues to spread via the "impartations" in Florida. Isn't that basically what is happening? Aren't the similarities too obvious to deny?

What spirit is all this of, my friends? Do we see these manifestations in the Bible? Or is this an alien spirit that has somehow invaded the church – masquerading as an "angel of light"?

A WORLDWIDE MOVEMENT

As J. Lee Grady pointed out, we now find a number of prominent leaders beginning to declare that the Florida revival will be one of the greatest revival movements in history. Some even see it as the beginning of a "new awakening".

The Elijah List claims that on New Year's Eve, for 2008, God told Bob Jones that "the third wave was coming." Todd asked Bob what the third wave was. He said that, *"Toronto was wave # 1, Pensacola was wave # 2, and the third wave is the 'Winds of Change' - this move of God. This move will be a global move, traveling with signs and wonders all over the world! The third wave is here!"*

Such predictions are now very common amongst the leadership circles associated with this revival. And it looks like they could well be right – as Todd Bentley's "Florida anointing" spreads right across the globe. As we have seen, reports are coming in from all over the USA, as well as Hawaii, England, New Zealand, Hong Kong – and pretty soon the whole world. It is truly everywhere.

But let me just put some serious questions before you at this point, my friends:

Isn't it possible, with all the dubious 'anointings' and angels and manifestations associated with Bentley's ministry, that what we are really seeing is a giant 'counterfeit' revival? Isn't it possible that if it continues to grow at the present rate, that it may literally become one of the great "delusions" of the Last Days – a great deception that has the power to actually deceive, if possible, the very elect?

Doesn't this particular movement, even more than other movements that have gone before, have many of the exact hallmarks of spiritual seduction and deception that are described in the Bible?

Could it actually become one of the "Great Deceptions" of the Last Days?

While it may be too early to answer many of these questions categorically, the fact remains that this is an hour when the people of God must hone their spiritual discernment as never before. We must be alert and watchful, for these are indeed the Last Days, and the devil is prowling around like a roaring lion, "seeking whom he may devour."

Friends, let us watch and pray.

CHAPTER THREE

WHAT IS REAL REVIVAL?

As someone who has been studying and writing on Revival history for many years, I'm sure you can understand why I have often been saddened by the corruption of the term "Revival" – and what it actually means. This book is all about "True and False Revival", so I guess it is high time that we look at the elements of TRUE Revival that have been seen again and again down the centuries.

Today, so few Christians seem to be aware of what really happens when God comes down (for that is what true Revival is – "GOD COMING DOWN"). When Moses came down from the mountain, he carried the holy presence and glory of God with him. The people wanted to run and hide! That is what true Revival has always been like. It is an invasion of the awesome holy presence of God – which is why the pattern of what happens in Revivals often repeats itself. Men's hearts are essentially the same in each generation – so God's holy presence has the same effect. Some get convicted, some want to run and hide, many cry loudly in repentance. Over and over, from the Book of Acts until now – we see the same things. And in a lot of ways, that makes it easier to discern the counterfeit from the real thing.

I am talking now about thousands of years of Revivals – where God has convicted men and women in the same way. Some people tell me, "Oh, it is going to be different this time." Yes, there will always be something "new" in each Revival, but essentially God deals with the hearts of men in a similar way each time. I really hate it when people call the latest froth-and-bubble fad that is sweeping through the church 'Revival'. It grates on me – it really does. We need to see people truly "cut to the heart" like on the day of Pentecost. We need piercing preaching like a Finney, a Wesley or a John-the-Baptist. And a "lukewarm" church needs these things more than anyone else.

Those who speak of Revival as a time of great celebration, ingathering and joy do not seem to realize that these things are the "fruit" that FOLLOW AFTER true Revival. True Revival itself is aimed at cleansing, purging and then empowering God's people. If they have fallen into a state of spiritual decline or lukewarmness, then the first thing that true Revival will bring is deep REPENTANCE. The whole idea is to see these Christians convicted and cleansed, so that they can once again become clean channels to bring God's blessing and salvation to a dying world – so that they can once again fully display His glory in the earth. True Revival brings God's children to their knees.

As one writer commented, Revival is "not the top blowing off, but rather the bottom falling out." And as Frank Bartleman (of the 'Azusa Street' Revival) wrote: "I received from God early in 1905 the following keynote to revival: 'The depth of revival will be determined exactly by the DEPTH OF THE SPIRIT OF REPENTANCE.' And this will obtain for all people, at all times." Anyone who has studied Revival history will say a big 'Amen' to Bartleman's words here.

It is not uncommon, in real Revivals, for people to be so stricken with conviction of sin by the Holy Spirit that they are literally unable to do anything except lie face-down and cry out to God for mercy, in the greatest distress, until assured by Him that they have received His forgiveness. (Usually, especially in the early stages of Revival, these will be CHRISTIANS who have been harboring sin of some kind in their lives). Sometimes they may even feel the need to confess their sin publicly before forgiveness and cleansing can take place. We must never forget that Revival is firstly aimed at the Christians. As history clearly shows, it is a flood of deep cleansing, repentance and empowering aimed at "reviving" God's people, so that they can bring in a mighty harvest.

The following is a description of some of the Revival prayer meetings that took place in the Welsh Revival of 1858-59 (typical of many Revivals): "It was in its terrors that the eternal became a reality to them first. They seemed plunged into depths of godly sorrow... For some weeks it was the voice of weeping and the sound of mourning that was heard in the meetings. The house was often so full of the divine presence that ungodly men trembled terror-stricken; and at the close, sometimes they fled as from some impending peril..."

One eyewitness said of the famous 1904 Welsh Revival that it was not the eloquence of Evan Roberts that broke men down, but his tears. "He would break down, crying bitterly for God to bend them, in an agony of prayer, the tears coursing down his cheeks, with his whole frame writhing. Strong men would break down and cry like children... a sound of weeping and wailing would fill the air."

Here is a typical extract from the autobiography of renowned Revivalist Charles Finney, concerning a meeting he held in one particularly ungodly place: "I had not spoken to them in this strain of direct application more than a quarter of an hour when all at once an awful solemnity seemed to settle down upon them. The congregation began to fall from their seats in every direction and cry for mercy. If I had had a sword in each hand I could not have cut them off their seats as fast as they fell. Indeed, nearly the whole congregation were either on their knees or prostrate in less than two minutes from this first shock that fell upon them. Everyone who was able to speak at all prayed for himself... Of course I was obliged to stop preaching, for they no longer paid any attention. I saw the old man who had invited me there to preach, sitting about in the middle of the house and looking around with utter amazement. I raised my voice almost to a scream to make him hear above the noise of the sobbing, and pointing to him said, 'Can't you pray?'..."

In this kind of genuine outpouring of the Holy Spirit, the tangible presence of God is very real. Frank Bartleman described one of the meetings during the Azusa Street Revival of 1906 as follows: "God came so wonderfully near us the very atmosphere of Heaven seemed to surround us. Such a divine 'weight of glory' was upon us we could only lie on our faces. For a long time we could hardly remain seated even. All would be on their faces on the floor, sometimes during the whole service. I was seldom able to keep from lying full length on the floor on my face."

This overwhelming sense of being in the awesome presence, the "shekinah glory" of a holy God, brings agonizing conviction of sin to those whose hearts are not right with Him, but also great rejoicing and true joy to the ones who know they have been washed clean. These extremes of great sorrow over sin, followed by genuine 'joy unspeakable', often bring accusations of emotionalism and hysteria from those who oppose the Revival. However, it has been found that deep and genuine moves of God that begin with deep conviction, and result in deep joy, have always produced sound and lasting fruit wherever they have occurred.

Many Revivals have resulted in such overwhelming joy, praise and jubilation in those newly forgiven, that bystanders have often been astonished at the shouts of glory to God, the unrestrained worship and singing, etc. It is important to remember however, that such "righteousness, peace and joy in the Holy Spirit" is only truly possible amongst those who have come to this place by way of brokenness and deep repentance. There must always be 'death' before there can be resurrection.

As Evan Roberts (of the 1904 Welsh Revival) said: "First, is there any sin in your past with which you have not honestly dealt, - not confessed to God? On your knees at once. Your past must be put away and cleansed. Second, is there anything in your life that is doubtful – anything you cannot decide whether it is good or evil?

Away with it. There must not be a trace of a cloud between you and God. Have you forgiven everybody – EVERYBODY? If not, don't expect forgiveness for your sins..." There can be no denying that deep repentance and prayer are truly the keys to genuine Revival. This has been the case with every previous outpouring, and it will undoubtably be the same with any coming one also.

REFORMATION – A NEW WINESKIN

Whenever God decides that it is vital that a new Revival be completely removed from the influence of the old leaders and the old church systems, then He will bring about not just a Revival, but a total "REFORMATION" – a complete 'leaving behind' of the old structures and leadership, etc. Really, the principle behind this is the same as that described by Jesus Himself in Luke 5:37-38: "And no one puts new wine into old wineskins, or else the new wine will burst the wineskins and be spilled, and the wineskins will be ruined. But new wine must be put into new wineskins..."

Church history often underlines the great folly of trying to preserve the new wine in the old skins. How many Revivals down the centuries have literally 'bled to death', simply because men have tried to cram the new wine into the old church systems and structures, etc? Often, all this has meant is that the Revival has been relatively short-lived, and has often failed to fully accomplish all that God had purposed for it. Really, the most effective and long-lived Revivals have been the ones that not only involved great outpourings of the Holy Spirit, but also the 'leaving behind' of old church systems (and all that went with them), and the formation of a new movement with new leaders, etc. Some well-known examples of this are the Great Reformation under Martin Luther, the Wesley Revivals of the eighteenth century, and the Salvation Army Revivals under William Booth (not to mention the original Book-of-Acts Revival itself).

All of these Revivals were really also Reformations, involving the leaving behind of the "old" systems, and the establishing of entirely new movements, with new leaders.

The desire to stay with the "old", to stick to what you know and feel comfortable with, to try and cram the new move of God into the existing structures, etc, is often a great temptation. However, this kind of 'comfort zone' mentality really has to go. It can be a deadly threat to the effectiveness and longevity of any Revival. If we are going to see a genuine move of God's Spirit in these last days that will truly sweep the world, then we had better get used to the idea, not only of the new wine, but also of the new wineskin that will go with it.

One thing that is important to remember is that many of the greatest Awakenings and Revivals in history have largely been "open-air" or street-based. Jesus himself mostly had an open-air ministry. So did John the Baptist – as well as the Book-of-Acts church in Jerusalem. And the First and Second Great Awakenings were largely "open-air" movements also. In many ways I believe that any coming Revival will have to be very similar to the Book of Acts – a simple, effective, largely house-based and street-based move of God. It will involve huge open-air meetings where the repentance preachers will speak (with true 'healings and miracles' following), and it will also involve small local gatherings of believers (usually from house to house), where local Christians will come together to pray, partake of the Lord's Supper, exercise spiritual gifts, etc: "Whenever you come together, each of you has a psalm, has a teaching, has a tongue, has a revelation, has an interpretation. Let all things be done for edification" (1 Cor 14:26).

"And they continued steadfastly in the apostles' doctrine and fellowship, in the breaking of bread, and in prayers. Then fear came upon every soul, and many wonders and signs were done through the apostles... And the Lord added to the church daily those who were being saved." (Acts 2:42-47).

REVIVAL LEADERS

In studying many past moves of God, it soon became apparent to me that there were often striking similarities between the various ones that God had chosen to lead His people in times of

Reformation and Revival. In fact, their spiritual lineage stretches way back to the "mighty men" of old – Joshua, Caleb, Moses, Gideon, Elijah, John the Baptist, etc – men of great daring and renown – all the way down through the apostles and on to Savonarola, Luther, Whitefield, Wesley, Edwards, Finney, William Booth, Evan Roberts, Jonathan Goforth, John Sung, Smith Wigglesworth, etc, etc. All were men who had "paid the price", who had spent much time alone in secret with God, and often years in the 'wilderness' before being anointed with power from on high and sent forth to loose God's people from their chains of bondage and sin. Suddenly they arrived, as if from nowhere, utterly fearless and with a searing message that pierced straight to the hearts of their hearers. This is the way it has always been and ever will be, with such "anointed ones" of God.

As A.W. Tozer has said, "God has always had His specialists... who appeared at critical moments in history to reprove, rebuke and exhort in the name of God and righteousness... Such a man was likely to be drastic, radical, possibly at times violent, and the curious crowd that gathered to watch him work soon branded him as extreme, fanatical, negative. And in a sense they were right. He was single-minded, severe, fearless, and these were the qualities the circumstances demanded. He shocked some, frightened others and alienated not a few, but he knew who had called him and what he was sent to do. His ministry was geared to the emergency, and that fact marked him out as different, a man apart."

The training ground for such men is often deep in the "wilderness" of brokenness, nothingness and death to self. As the historian D'Aubigne wrote, "A great work of God is never accomplished by the natural strength of man. It is from the dry bones, the darkness and the dust of death, that God is pleased to select the instruments by means of which He designs to scatter over the earth His light, regeneration and life."

Yet another writer has observed, "In the various crises that have occurred in the history of the church, men have come to the front who have manifested a holy recklessness that astonished their fellows. When Luther nailed his theses to the door of the cathedral at Wittemburg, cautious men were astonished at his audacity. When John Wesley ignored all church restrictions and religious propriety and preached in the fields and by-ways, men declared his reputation was ruined. So it has been in all ages... An utter recklessness concerning men's opinions and other consequences is the only attitude that can meet the exigencies of the present times."

Such men as these were often the most controversial figures of their day. They were loved by some and utterly loathed by others. They were usually perceived as a threat to the status quo, the church "establishment", and so were often treated with great suspicion – even hatred – by those in power. These were men who had battled through in prayer, right into the very throneroom of God. There they had tasted of the heavenly glory, and had been imbued with a vision and a passion far beyond mere words. And now they were dangerous men – men on fire with love and devotion toward a holy God. Never again would they be satisfied with a church that did not fully display His glory and His majesty to a dying world. Never again would they allow their Saviour to be left "wounded in the house of His friends."

These Reformers and Revivalists were men who had surrendered all to God, who had been willing to pay any price to see God arise and scatter His enemies in the earth. They had willingly allowed themselves to be humbled and broken by Him, so that they might one day become true instruments of His glory. They were truly dead to self, dead to sin, "dead to the world and all its toys, its idle pomp and fading joys". They were alive only to Jesus, and His word burned in their hearts as a consuming fire, and in their mouths as a two-edged sword.

REVIVAL PREACHING

As we have seen, it is a well-known fact that the old Revivalists used to often preach searchingly and fearlessly on "sin, righteousness and judgment". There is a very good reason for this:

Jesus had specifically stated that the Holy Spirit would CONVICT of these very things – "sin, righteousness and judgment"! (Jn 16:8). The whole purpose of these men's preaching was to unleash the convicting power of the Holy Spirit upon their hearers. They aimed to thoroughly awaken the consciences of the people. Welsh Revivalist Humphrey Jones once urged a young preacher: "...to preach with severity and conviction; aiming continually at the conscience; charging the people with their sins to their very face; having no regard for men's good or bad opinions; and avoiding the exhibition of self during the delivery of your sermon." Now THAT is Revival preaching!

These men would wield God's word under a mighty anointing, not as some kind of blunt weapon to bludgeon people with, but rather as an incisive, precision instrument, a "sharp, two-edged sword", piercing deep into men's hearts, exposing hidden sins, motives and desires, and bringing true godly sorrow and deep repentance. What these preachers were looking for was a "broken heart and a contrite spirit". As with Peter on the day of Pentecost, they preached with a view to seeing men 'cut to the heart', for only then could they be sure that the resulting repentance would be both truly deep and truly lasting.

This has almost always been the character of true Revival preaching, from the days of the apostles right down to the present. On the day of Pentecost it was Peter accusing the Jews to their faces of 'crucifying the Messiah' that caused them to be cut to the heart, and to cry out, "Men and brethren, what shall we do?" (Acts 2:36-37). And the record states that three thousand people were converted that day after hearing this one Spirit-fired sermon. Later in the book of Acts we read of Paul's fearless preaching to governor Felix: "And as he reasoned of righteousness, self control, and the judgment to come, Felix was afraid..." (Acts 24:25). And for another Scriptural example of this kind of bold, convicting preaching, we can turn to the martyr Stephen: "'You stiff-necked and uncircumcised in heart and ears! You always resist the Holy Spirit: as your fathers did, so do you.'" (Acts 7:51-53). There are many further examples of this kind of preaching throughout the

New Testament (in the ministries of Jesus and John the Baptist, for instance).

Revival preaching is almost never designed to be deliberately offensive. However it is often extremely direct and utterly fearless. And, as one writer has noted, "fearless" preaching of this kind seems calculated to produce either deep conviction or "the bitterest animosity" (often both)! The old Revivalists were men of enormous Godly authority, and they used God's word as a sword to 'lay siege' to the strongholds of sin, compromise and religion that were binding His people. This was never 'comfortable' preaching (for "sin, righteousness and judgment" are not comfortable subjects). However, these men well knew that "the fear of the Lord is the beginning of wisdom" (Pr 9:10). And they preached it as such.

As Martin Luther said: "I was born to fight devils and factions. It is my business to remove obstructions, to cut down thorns, to fill up quagmires, and to open and make straight paths. But if I must have some failing let me rather speak the truth with too great severity than once to act the hypocrite and conceal the truth." And the well-known Revivalist Charles Finney said of one typical meeting: "The Spirit of God came upon me with such power that it was like opening a battery upon them. For more than an hour, and perhaps for an hour and a half, the word of God came through me to them in a manner that I could see was carrying all before it. It was a fire and a hammer breaking the rock, and as a sword that was piercing to the dividing asunder of soul and spirit. I saw that a general conviction was spreading over the whole congregation. Many of them could not hold up their heads."

Renowned eighteenth century Revivalist Jonathan Edwards (preacher of the famous sermon, "Sinners in the hands of an angry God") noted that the two outstanding features of genuine Revival were great conviction followed by great praise and rejoicing. The following are the characteristics that he himself observed: "(a) An extraordinary sense of the awful majesty, greatness and holiness of God so as sometimes to overwhelm soul and body, a sense of the piercing, all-seeing eye of God so as to sometimes take away the bodily strength; and an extraordinary view of the infinite terribleness of the wrath of God, together with the ineffable misery of sinners exposed to this wrath. (b) Especially longing after these two things; to be more perfect in humility and adoration... The person felt a great delight in singing praises to God and Jesus Christ, and longing that this present life may be as it were one continued song of praise to God..."

The Revivalists of old often preached under such an incredible anointing that the house would be literally full of the wailing cries and sobs of those stricken by God's Spirit. One eyewitness wrote of Savonarola's preaching that it caused "such terror and alarm, such sobbing and tears that people passed through the streets without speaking, more dead than alive"! Some modern Christians, totally unused to this kind of preaching, might say that such an emphasis on "sin, righteousness and judgment" is way over the top. However, in circumstances such as those found in today's church, this kind of preaching is EXACTLY what is needed. This is why God has so often seen fit to raise up and employ this kind of preaching in conditions very similar to today.

The old Revivalists were so full of God's presence, so saturated with His glory, so endued with power from on high, that Revival literally followed them wherever they went. They would never have dared to preach the way they did without this anointing (for 'the letter kills but the Spirit gives life'). But how exactly did they obtain such a mighty anointing? Well, as most of the old records show, it was largely through agonizing, prevailing PRAYER that they had broken through into this place of real "Revival" power in their ministry.

REVIVAL PRAYING

Charles Finney said, "... unless I had the spirit of prayer I could do nothing. If I lost the spirit of grace and supplication even for a day or an hour I found myself unable to preach with power and efficiency, or to win souls by personal conversation." Frank

Bartleman wrote: "At night I could scarcely sleep for the spirit of prayer... Prayer literally consumed me." And D.M. McIntyre stated: "Before the great revival in Gallneukirchen broke out, Martin Boos spent hours and days and often nights in lonely agonies of intercession. Afterwards, when he preached, his words were as flame, and the hearts of the people as grass."

This was urgent, anointed, Spirit-fired praying, led and inspired by God. The old Revivalists used to speak of the spirit of prayer being "outpoured" upon them. They spoke of weeping, agonizing, pleading, wrestling, 'travailing' in prayer. The whole reason that these Revival preachers were so saturated with the glory and the presence of God was because they had truly broken through, right into His very throneroom in prayer, and had spent much time communing with Him there. Deep repentance, daring faith, and 'agonizing', Spirit-fired prayer have always been the keys to genuine Revival in any age (and this, of course, applies to everybody, not just to those in ministry).

As history shows, the church can only ever expect true Revival when at least a remnant of God's people truly get DESPERATE – desperate about the backslidden state of the church, desperate about the lukewarmness within them and all around them, desperate about sin and compromise, desperate about the fact that GOD IS NOT GLORIFIED, that He is not truly LORD of His church, that His words are mocked and largely seen as irrelevant by a dying world. Revival will come when God's people truly humble themselves, when they replace their 'positive imaging' ("Rise up, you people of power", etc), with the reality of James' lament: "Be afflicted, and mourn, and weep: let your laughter be turned to mourning, and your joy to heaviness. Humble yourselves in the sight of the Lord, and He shall lift you up" (Ja 4:9-10, KJV). We all need to stop playing games and get serious with God. I really believe He is calling us to get 'desperate' about our plight before Him.

In the coming Revival, as with all Revivals, God will no doubt raise up particular intercessors who will 'specialize' in prayer. But really, such praying is for everyone. It was Matthew Henry who said, "When God intends great mercy for His people, the first thing He does is set them a-praying." And Leonard Ravenhill wrote that "the man who can get believers to praying would, under God, usher in the greatest revival that the world has ever known." God will often gather His people together (at least in twos and threes, and often more) to pray down a Revival – just like Pentecost itself. As A.T. Pierson wrote, "From the day of Pentecost, there has been not one great spiritual awakening in any land which has not begun in a union of prayer, though only among two or three; no such outward, upward movement has continued after such prayer meetings declined."

John Wesley said: "Have you any days of fasting and prayer? Storm the throne of grace and persevere therein, and mercy will come down." And Charles Finney declared: "Revival comes from heaven when heroic souls enter the conflict determined to win or die – or if need be, to win and die!" Brothers, sisters, we need to get DESPERATE about Revival!

REVIVAL IN THE COMMUNITY

Once the Christians who heed God's call have been through the fire of His refining, purifying and cleansing, and have received His mighty anointing, then it becomes time for the community at large to experience this great invasion of God's Revival power also. This is when the 'harvest' will truly begin. This is the time for the church to fearlessly invade Satan's kingdom under a mighty anointing, 'releasing the captives' as they go. For those who have experienced God's cleansing and forgiveness, such a time can literally be like "heaven on earth". One writer described Revival as being "a community saturated with God". And Jonathan Edwards said of the 1735 New England Revival, "The town seemed to be full of the presence of God. It was never so full of love, or so full of joy; and yet, so full of distress as it was then."

When Revival spreads out into the community in this way, it is not uncommon for bars to be transformed into prayer meetings, for large numbers of notorious criminals to be converted, and for judges to be left without cases to put to trial! Such is the impact of a mighty general outpouring of the Spirit of God. This is the kind of result that we can expect in any coming great move of God also. Really, these kinds of things are what the church should be seeing on a large scale all the time, but at the moment the 'channels' of such blessing are almost completely blocked by sin and compromise within the church.

REVIVAL PIONEERS

How can individual Christians help pave the way for a powerful move of God's Spirit? How can they help Revival to come down? The answer is really very simple: To be truly ready to play a part in any new move of God, it is necessary to first experience PERSONAL REVIVAL in your own life. In other words, it is necessary to have already been "revived" yourself. This "personal Revival" process involves seeking God with all your heart, ridding your life of any 'cloud' that may be coming between you and God (and asking Him to reveal anything else that He wants dealt with), brokenness, and 'agonizing' prayer (that God would outpour His Spirit upon you and fill you with His faith, His love, His word, His anointing, etc). As Robert Murray McCheyne said, "a holy minister is an awful weapon in the hands of God."

Before any Revival begins, God spends much time (often many years) training His "pioneers", preparing them (often in some secluded spiritual backwater) for the day when His Spirit will be outpoured and they will explode out of the wilderness and onto the world stage with a piercing message and a holy boldness that will kindle fire in the hearts of all who hear them. As Frank Bartleman wrote of the Pentecostal pioneers who were gathered for the Azusa Street outpouring: "They were largely called and prepared for years... They had been burnt out, tried and proven... They had walked with God and learned deeply of His Spirit. These were pioneers, 'shock troops', the Gideon's three hundred, to spread the fire around the world. Just as the disciples had been prepared by

Jesus." He also observed that, "A body must be prepared, in repentance and humility, for every outpouring of the Spirit."

As Arthur Booth-Clibborn wrote: "The company in the upper room, upon whom Pentecost fell, had paid for it the highest price. In this they approached as near as possible to Him who had paid the supreme price in order to send it. Do we ever really adequately realize how utterly lost to this world, how completely despised, rejected and outcast was that company?... Their Calvary was complete, and so a complete Pentecost came to match it. The latter will resemble the former in completeness. We may, therefore, each of us say to ourselves: As thy cross, so will thy Pentecost be."

It is my belief that God is still looking for Christians to join the ranks of His "Gideon's three hundred" for a true Revival: "I sought for a man among them who would make a wall, and stand in the gap before Me on behalf of the land..." (Ez 22:30). "For the eyes of the LORD run to and fro throughout the whole earth, to show Himself strong on behalf of those whose heart is loyal to Him" (2 Ch 16:9). Are YOU willing to become one of those who "stand in the gap" before the Lord? Are you willing to suffer the reproach and the rejection of others as you take your stand with Him? And are you truly willing to pay the price, to 'take up your cross' no matter what the cost? The Bible tells us that Jesus was "a man of sorrows, and acquainted with grief." It is only those who are prepared and praying who will be involved in such a Revival from the beginning. And for the pioneers, in many ways this will mean "loving not their lives unto the death". A true pioneer's most pressing desire will be to SEE GOD GLORIFIED in every conceivable way. This has always been the purest motive for desiring Revival in any age. And I believe that God is still seeking those who will stand in the gap before Him for this present generation. Tell me, friend, might you be one of these?

It is my hope that after reading this chapter, people will be able to clearly see the difference between revivals that are true and those that are false. One is centered around the CROSS and DEEP REPENTANCE and HOLINESS and DEATH TO SELF – as well as FORGIVENESS, CLEANSING and the INFILLING of the HOLY SPIRIT – who is the Spirit of "HOLINESS". The other is centered around excitement and soulishness and the seeking after of 'experiences' for their own sake – often with a selfish agenda – "Bless me God", "Give me more" – rather than a focus on GETTING RIGHT WITH GOD. I hope this distinction is now becoming more and more clear.

For those who want to develop an even deeper understanding of true Revival, I highly recommend the following books:

- 'Why Revival Tarries' by Leonard Ravenhill

- 'Azusa Street' by Frank Bartleman

- 'The Autobiography of Charles Finney'

- 'In the Day of Thy Power' by Arthur Wallace

- 'Revival' by Winkie Pratney

- and there are many more.

CHAPTER FOUR

MANIFESTATIONS IN REVIVALS

One thing that it is very important to realize in our discussion is that "unusual" things occur in true Revivals – not just false ones. And this often causes a great deal of alarm and controversy.

In true Revivals we often find God Himself doing unexpected things at times – but also the devil frantically trying to introduce counterfeits as fast as he can. Thus even genuine Revivals can tend to be "messy" affairs – especially around the fringes. This is a very important thing to remember.

In fact, the bigger the cloud of confusion, rumors and false manifestations surrounding a true Revival, the happier the devil will be. One of the devil's favorite tricks in times of Revival is to push some of the 'pro-Revival' ministries to real extremes in their preaching and ministering, etc, so as to discredit the whole move of God because of them. As Frank Bartleman wrote, "Man always adds to the message God has given. This is Satan's chief way to discredit and destroy it. Both Luther and Wesley had the same difficulties to contend with. And so has every God given revival... The message generally suffers more from its friends than from its foes." John Wesley once prayed, "Oh, Lord, send us the old revival, without the defects; but if this cannot be, send it – with all its defects. We must have the revival."

As you know, we have already spent a good deal of time in this book looking at counterfeit manifestations and false experiences. However, it is important to remind ourselves of the "unusual" physical responses that sometimes occur when the true Holy Spirit descends upon an individual as well. As I said, this has often been the most controversial aspect of any Revival. For instance, imagine if masses of people suddenly started "falling down" at some meetings in your town. (This has happened in many Revivals). Would some church members be opposed to these 'fallings'? Would there be controversy and alarm and opposition? Certainly! And remember, when the Holy Spirit descends there can be other emotional outbursts (just like on the Day of Pentecost) such as tremendous cryings of distress over sin or 'trembling' under the fear of God, outbursts of joyous forgiveness, mass speaking in 'tongues', dreams, visions, dancing for joy, etc.

The key is whether or not these things have a sense of God's holiness and truth about them – and whether these encounters are producing good fruit (i.e., godly results in people's lives) such as holy living and a greater hunger for God. We cannot just automatically write something off because it is "unusual". We have to 'test the spirits'.

For Revival leaders, the whole issue of counterfeits can be a very touchy area. If they are happening on the fringes, but are not causing large-scale problems, then it can be best for the leaders not to draw too much attention to them. (Attempting to loudly correct relatively small-scale problems can sometimes make the people overly suspicious of ANYTHING unusual, thus making it hard for the Holy Spirit to work as well). However, if these counterfeits are flooding in on a large scale, it may be necessary for the leaders to bring open correction, using all the authority that God has given them.

I believe that the leadership in any true Revival will be very wary of encouraging soulishness in any way. I certainly can't imagine them using the kind of "tugging at the heart-strings" techniques so often seen today. All that is showy, all that is soulish, all that is shallow and that would wrap people up in a warm, positive, "feel-good" cocoon – all this God hates. And yet this kind of thing has become all too common in recent years. In my experience, very few Christians even seem to be able to tell this kind of Christianity from the real thing any more.

True Revival ministries will detest this kind of soulishness, hype and emotional manipulation. Their preaching (and their singing) will certainly not be in demonstration of personality, cleverness or showmanship, but rather, "in demonstration of the Spirit and of power" (1 Cor 2:4). However, despite this, I have no doubt that any true Revival today would be accused of emotionalism and hysteria, just like all those that have gone before.

A MANIA FOR 'EXPERIENCES'

When the "manifestations" movement invaded the church in the mid-1990's, there were a lot of claims being made that it was somehow "just like Revivals of the past." I have to tell you, as someone who has been studying and writing on Revivals for years, this was an absolutely absurd claim. In fact, what this bizarre new movement most closely resembled was the COUNTERFEITS that often used to invade real Revivals – sometimes corrupting and destroying them. As the well-known Revivalist John Wesley declared, "At the first, revival is true and pure, but after a few weeks watch for counterfeits."

It is a very significant fact that two of the greatest Revivals in history were pretty-much derailed and destroyed by "manifestation" movements that swept through at the time, while another had a very close call indeed. Both the Great Awakening and the 1904 Welsh Revival were basically destroyed in this way, while the Second Great Awakening in Kentucky came very close to shipwreck. Yes, I will repeat what I just said: Two of these massive moves of God were virtually ruined and finished-off by a flood of bizarre "manifestations" that swept through during the Revival. Many other moves of God have also had to contend with similar manifestations trying to get in. A lot of well-known Revivalists have commented on how difficult it was to keep the Revival on the rails and prevent the devil from bringing these kinds of things in.

This is a major reason why many Revivals have ended well before their time infiltrated, swamped or stymied by the dirty tactics of the enemy. Many moves of God, instead of lasting decades as they could have, only lasted a matter of a few years (if that). When studying history it is alarming to see how successful the devil has been at destroying Revivals through flooding them with counterfeits, deceiving spirits, bizarre manifestations, disputes and excesses, etc. This is not a front-on attack as such, but rather an "attack from within", where the bizarre goings-on that arise from within the Revival either swamp it or bring discredit on the whole thing, eventually bringing it to a grinding halt. Satan can often finish Revivals off very quickly when he gets them to this stage. As John Wesley said: "Be not alarmed that Satan sows tares among the wheat of Christ. It has ever been so, especially on any remarkable outpouring of the Spirit; and ever will be, until the devil is chained for a thousand years. Till then he will always ape, and endeavor to counteract the work of the Spirit of Christ."

False manifestations are often caused by believers seeking 'touches', blessings or experiences, rather than seeking God for His own sake. It is very dangerous for Christians to seek anything but a deeper and purer relationship with Christ Himself. Any seeking after mere touches or experiences is really nothing but "soulishness", and can result in great spiritual deception. Some of the false manifestations that result are merely fleshly, while others can be downright demonic – especially if they involve a 'casting off of restraint' or a kind of "wildness". Sometimes, in extreme cases, it is possible for whole movements to be given over to these kinds of counterfeit manifestations. As the renowned revivalist Charles Finney stated, "God's Spirit leads men by the intelligence, not through mere impressions... I have known some cases where persons have rendered themselves highly ridiculous, have greatly injured their own souls, and the cause of God, by giving themselves up to an enthusiastic and fanatical following of impressions."

As we spoke about earlier, in both the First and Second Great Awakenings, as well as in some of the Pentecostal Revivals of more recent times, it has often been common for people to "fall down under the power of God". As you can imagine, this caused a great deal of controversy. But please note that the Great Awakenings were mostly about conviction, repentance and holiness – not the seeking after of 'manifestations'. This is a true hallmark of Revival. As Pentecostal pioneer Frank Bartleman (of the Azusa Street Revival) wrote: "Many are willing to seek 'power' from every battery they can lay their hands on, in order to perform miracles... A true 'Pentecost' will produce a mighty conviction for sin, a turning to God. False manifestations produce only excitement and wonder... Any work that exalts the Holy Ghost or the 'gifts' above Jesus will finally land up in fanaticism."

As touched on before, genuine manifestations that have taken place in true Revivals include trembling or weeping under the fear of God – or afterward (when repentance and forgiveness have taken place) outbursts of joyous praise and thanksgiving, etc. All of this is perfectly normal. Spiritual gifts such as tongues and prophecy, and all kinds of Biblical phenomena are to be expected; for as we have noted, God Himself sometimes does 'strange' things. But as I said, it is when these phenomena move into being "weird" or ugly that we need to take great care.

Now, let us take a look at the exact manifestations that flooded into three of the greatest Revivals in history.

The leaders of the First Great Awakening, both in America and Europe, had a number of run-ins with counterfeit manifestations. It was an ever-present danger that most of them were aware of. For instance, here is what Jonathan Edwards wrote concerning the supposedly 'heavenly' trances that members of his congregation were entering into under the ministry of Samuel Buelle (a visiting preacher): "But when the people were raised to this height, Satan took the advantage, and his interposition in many instances soon became very apparent; and a great deal of caution and pains were found necessary to keep the people, many of them from running wild."

And speaking of things in Europe that seemed likely to bring the true Revival into disrepute and danger, John Wesley wrote: "It is chiefly among these enormous mountains that so many have been awakened, justified, and soon after perfected in love; but even while they are full of love, Satan strives to push many of them to extravagance. This appears in several instances: ... Some of them, perhaps many, scream all together as loud as they possibly can... Several drop down as dead; and are as stiff as a corpse; but in a while they start up, and cry, "Glory! glory!" perhaps twenty times together. Just so do the French Prophets, and very lately the Jumpers in Wales, bring the real work into contempt." Historian Henry Baird wrote of these so-called French Prophets: "Such persons would suddenly fall backward, and while extended at full length on the ground, undergo strange and apparently involuntary contortions." And George Lavington wrote of them: "I don't remember any of these laughing-fits among Papists. But they were very common among the French Prophets in their agitations."

As I said, most of the Revival leaders were aware of the dangers of counterfeits and fanaticism flooding in, especially John Wesley in England, who mentioned such things in his journal on a number of occasions. Please note his concern in the above quote that these things were bringing "the real work into contempt." Exactly! That is precisely what they do.

In America, the most serious damage to the First Great Awakening occurred under pro-Revival preachers such as James Davenport and others who gained great notoriety for themselves with their excessive preaching and behavior – which definitely helped to bring an end to the whole Revival. As the Boston Evening Post wrote of Davenport: "He has no knack at raising the Passions, but by a violent straining of his Lungs, and the most extravagant wreathings of his Body, which at the same time that it creates

Laughter and Indignation in the most, occasions great meltings, screamings, crying, swooning and Fits in some others... they look'd more like a Company of Bacchanalians after a mad Frolick than sober Christians who had been worshipping God..." These and other goings-on soon brought such controversy upon the whole Revival, that the Great Awakening ended in a deluge of bitter arguments and disputes. Surely one of the devil's all-time favorite methods for killing Revivals stone-dead. It had lasted just three years.

James Davenport actually made a public apology for these excesses in 1744, but by then it was far too late and the Revival was over.

There is no doubt that the Great Awakening had already done tremendous good by this stage, but what might have been accomplished if it had been able to continue for another decade or longer? This is something we will never know, for the devil used his usual tricks to take the legs right out from under it. And the end came very quickly after that.

Just over 50 years later, the Second Great Awakening centered in Kentucky came very close to suffering a similar fate. As usual, in the beginning this was a tremendous move of conviction and repentance. And so it largely remained at the start. People would fall down under great conviction of sin, piercing the air with their cries. Then, after a time they would experience such forgiveness that they were flooded with joy. All of this is perfectly normal in Revivals. But after about a year, as the Revival reached Cane Ridge and the camp-meetings became much larger, some truly bizarre manifestations began to flood in, and for awhile they came to almost dominate the Revival. This came very close to shipwrecking the entire movement in the Western states.

As noted Revival historian Keith J. Hardman writes: "Cane Ridge also witnessed the beginning of excesses that had been generally condemned... ever since the wild antics and frenzies of James Davenport and others had brought discredit on the Great

Awakening of New England in the 1740's. Excesses, or 'enthusiasms,' were viewed with great distaste by most prorevival evangelists..."

Fortunately for the Kentucky Revival, these more bizarre manifestations began to die out before they could do irreparable damage. But it was a very close call. As Hardman continues: "At later camp meetings shouting, crying, and falling down were the only physical reactions to rousing preaching. With the release of tidal waves of feeling in those early camp meetings, however, convulsive physical 'exercises' became somewhat common. Hysterical laughter, occasional trances, the 'barking' exercise and the 'jerks'..."

Here is how T.W. Caskey, an eyewitness, described these earlier manifestations which had almost ruined the Revival: "The whole congregation by some inexplicable nervous action would sometimes be thrown into side-splitting convulsions of laughter and when it started, no power could check or control it until it ran its course. At other times the nervous excitement set the muscles to twitching and jerking at a fearful rate and finally settle down to regular, straight-forward dancing. Like the 'Holy Laugh' it was simply ungovernable until it ran its course. When a man started laughing, dancing, shouting or jerking, it was impossible for him to stop until exhausted nature broke down in a death-like swoon..." The same writer goes on to tell how a number of people slowly began to question whether such things really were the work of the Holy Spirit. They began to search the Scriptures and 'test the spirits' a lot more than they had been, and these more bizarre manifestations began to die out. This was very fortunate, as they had come close to bringing disrepute and disaster upon the whole movement. The Revival was able to sweep on without them after that. And it was to continue for another six years – maybe longer. Unlike the First Great Awakening, these kinds of excesses had not managed to kill the Revival stone dead.

However, it is a fact that these early Kentucky manifestations were notorious for decades afterwards, tainting the whole concept of 'revival' for many people. Even modern music historian Steve Turner writes of the Kentucky camp-meetings that the crowds would "go into trances, writhe on the ground and even bark like dogs." He doesn't mention that originally these gatherings had been for strong preaching and deep repentance. You see, it is often the bizarre and damaging elements that are remembered the longest. What a shame.

History shows that such counterfeits and excesses have often flooded in towards the end of a true Revival, when the devil has been trying to get in and completely destroy or discredit it. This is precisely what happened to the 1904 Welsh Revival.

As many Christians know, Wales in 1904-1905 was truly aflame for God. This was one of the most powerful Revivals of all time. The bars and taverns were emptied, the judges were left with few (if any) criminal cases to try, and tens of thousands were converted in a matter of months. The Revival was being reported in newspapers around the world.

But the young leader, Evan Roberts, was suffering badly under the strain of it all. He was just 27 years old. Roberts apparently got the idea from somewhere that he was "stealing glory from God" by being so prominent in the Revival. He had already suffered several minor breakdowns under the pressure. This time he hid himself away for good – stating that he was giving his life over to prayer and seclusion. The Revival had only been going for about a year, and without Roberts there was no-one with the leadership or anointing to keep the counterfeits out and keep the whole thing on the rails. It very quickly began to fall apart.

In the months and years that followed, the devil flooded the whole thing with deceptions and false manifestations on such a scale that this Revival probably had the "messiest" ending in history. It was to be the last Revival that Wales would ever have – right up to the present day. What a disaster. But at least one hundred thousand converts remained steadfast.

Several years later, Evan Roberts and Jesse Penn-Lewis co-authored a book called "War on the Saints" to warn against all the counterfeits and deceptions that they were seeing in the aftermath of the Revival. It is a disturbing book which probably places too much emphasis on the devil, but vividly describes many counterfeit manifestations and how to avoid being deceived by them.

The book makes some very wise observations about how deception enters in. Here is a typical extract: "... these demons hover round the soul, and make strange suggestions to the mind of something odd, or outlandish, or contrary to common sense or decent taste. They make these suggestions under the profession of being the Holy Ghost. They fan the emotions, and produce a strange, fictitious exhilaration, which is simply their bait to get into some faculty of the soul... another person said he felt like rolling on the floor, and groaning and pulling the chairs around, but he distinctly perceived that the impulse to do so had something wild in it; and a touch of self display contrary to the gentleness and sweetness of Jesus; and, as quick as he saw it was an attack of a false spirit, he was delivered. But another man had the same impulse, and fell down groaning and roaring, beating the floor with his hands and feet, and the demon entered into him as an angel of light, and got him to think that his conduct was of the Holy Ghost, and it became a regular habit in the meetings he attended, until he would ruin every religious meeting he was in... The effects of being influenced by this sort of demon is manifold, and plainly legible to a well-poised mind. They cause people to run off into things that are odd and foolish, unreasonable and indecent..."

The authors also make the following very crucial statement in the same book: "The false conception of 'surrender' as yielding the body to supernatural power, with the mind ceasing to act, is the HIGHEST SUBTLETY OF THE ENEMY." Charles Finney made very similar statements in his own day.

Now, as we have seen clearly in this chapter, there is absolutely NO WAY that Revivalists such as Finney, Wesley, Bartleman,

Roberts, etc, would have condoned or praised a "manifestations" movement such as the one we have seen in the last fifteen years – with very little emphasis on repentance or holiness – but rather on bizarre and outlandish manifestations, etc. In fact, what we are seeing today is whole movements made up of the very things that they were trying to KEEP OUT of their own Revivals! It is the "counterfeits" that have taken over. I find it ridiculous in the extreme when modern writers try to prove the validity of these manifestations by pointing to past Revivals and saying, "These things happened back then too." Yes – they did! They happened when counterfeits and excesses were trying to flood in and ruin real moves of God. All the great revivalists would tell you so.

As we have seen, it seems that many similar deceptions are very prevalent in the Prophetic movement, the Charismatic movement and others today. In fact, as a student of Revival history I would have to say that both of these movements now display many of the hallmarks of "fallen" moves of God. Don't we realize that much of the deception prophesied for the Last Days must clearly arise from WITHIN THE CHURCH? Surely much worse is to come, but I believe we already see signs of this "great deception" working in our midst today.

In the times we live in, it is essential for Christians to hone their discernment as much as possible. I myself certainly believe in the moving of the Holy Spirit and the gifts of the Spirit and true signs and wonders from God. And I cannot doubt that such things will have a definite part to play in any true Revival – just as they did in the Book of Acts – which is full of healings and miracles of every kind. But the Bible does clearly state that the Last Days are an age of deception. And in times like these a real Revival can only survive if it is deeply grounded in the truth, the holiness and the discernment of God.

CHAPTER FIVE

THE FIVE KEYS TO DISCERNMENT

In criticizing books like this one, some Christians claim that any correction or questioning of ministries should always be done PRIVATELY – and only to the leaders concerned – never in public. (It is important to note that many such approaches have indeed been made to Todd Bentley and other Prophetic leaders over the years). But I am afraid I cannot agree that public deception is only to be opposed behind closed doors. It seems to me that false teaching would thrive in such an environment. In Scripture we see clearly that there are occasions when private correction is appropriate, and other occasions when a more public airing is necessary. There is the quiet "Matthew 18" approach, and then there are others.

We must not forget that in the New Testament the elders were commanded to correct severely (Titus 1:13) and to rebuke for sin publicly (1 Tim 5:20), though in 2 Tim 2:24-26 they were instructed to correct with 'meekness'. Remember, the apostle Paul rebuked Peter publicly in Galatians 2 for his hypocrisy, Jesus rebuked Peter openly in Matthew, and He even whipped the sellers out of the temple publicly in Mark (for making God's house a 'den of thieves'). In extreme cases the apostle Paul actually wrote to everyone that he was turning people over to Satan for correction (see 1 Cor 5 and 1 Tim 1:20). The Bible is very clear that one of our major tasks is to "expose" the deeds of darkness (Eph 5:11). In 1 Cor 4:21 Paul asks the people, "Shall I come to you with a rod, or in love?" The same apostle used 'boldness' in 2 Cor 10:1 and said that he would not spare anyone in 2 Cor 13:1-2.

Many Christians insist on applying Matt 18:15-17 to every situation. But what about false teachers? The above passage in Matt 18 says that if my brother "sins against me" then I should go to him privately about it – then with one or two witnesses – and then to the whole church if he does not repent. This is a very important process for resolving issues where a brother has sinned against me personally. But what about FALSE TEACHING of a serious nature? What if it is spreading or starting to infect entire sections of the body of Christ? Is it still just a "private matter"?

My understanding is that in the New Testament we NEVER see Jesus or the apostles treating false teaching as a "Matt 18" scenario. We see them publicly rebuking and correcting – trying to arrest the 'cancer' before it spreads any further. This is an act of LOVE towards the body. It is trying to stop the damage before too many precious sheep are harmed. False teaching and false prophets are never treated "nicely" or "sweetly" in the New Testament! (By the way, I am not advocating today's "heresy hunters", whom I believe often go about things with entirely the wrong spirit. But I am just laying down a few biblical guidelines here).

This is certainly an important issue in these Last Days, when we are told that false prophets and false teachers will 'abound', and that the deception will become so great that "if possible it would deceive the very elect". It is vital that we get a grasp of what is at stake here. The false teachers and false prophets in Acts were rebuked very bluntly, and Paul even "named names" in some of his letters to the churches. So surely we cannot continue to claim that this is all a "Matt 18" situation? Surely it is more serious than that – and requires a more drastic response?

So what are some of the key ways that we can spot false prophets and false teachers when we come across them? What are some general guidelines to help us?

THE 5 KEYS TO DISCERNMENT

Some people say that knowing Scripture is the only real key to discernment that we need. And yes – Scripture is very important – especially in exposing false doctrine. But it is not only doctrines or teachings that are the greatest danger today. It is just as likely to be false 'anointings' or spirits – perhaps even "lying signs and wonders". And we may need more than just a good understanding of Scripture to spot these things. Remember, a lot of the people caught up in the "manifestations mania" that we described in the last chapter actually know their Bible quite well. And yet they could still be deceived. So what are the things that can help us avoid deception in similar situations?

Some of the most basic keys to discernment that God has shown me are as follows:

(1) Know your HOLY GOD intimately. (When you have seen His glory, His holiness and His love – by drawing close to Him in prayer – then you can usually see through any counterfeits because you know the "real thing" so well).

(2) Know your Bible. It is very important to be able to spot teachings that are either extra-biblical or directly opposed to what the Scriptures teach. However, it is important to remember that the Scribes and Pharisees were extremely learned in the Scriptures and yet they missed the very Messiah that was prophesied! So knowing the Bible is important – especially for doctrinal issues – but we need to be able to "discern the spirits" also.

(3) Be a "lover of truth". This is very crucial. Are you someone who will actually stand up for Truth – even against the crowd? Or do you remain silent even when you are convinced something is very wrong?

(4) Purity of heart and Humility. Many deceptions only appeal to

us because there is something inside us that "wants" to believe them. They are seductive because of darkness and wrong motives in our own lives. We must search our hearts and root these out.

(5) The 'inner witness' of the Holy Spirit. We must learn to never over-ride this "still small voice", as it will save us from deception again and again (more on this below).

Did you know that even an unbeliever can often spot a con-man or a snake-oil salesman? They get a kind-of "gut feeling" about such things. And they are often right! In fact, they are often less gullible than the Christians! (Because we are told in the church – "Do not judge", 'Touch not the Lord's anointed', "You have a critical spirit if you do not join in", etc. This is the very reason why Christians are often the most gullible and easily deceived). We need to realize that the Bible says to "test the spirits" and warns very strongly that the Last Days will be a time of "seducing spirits" and great deception. So how can we become more alert to these things?

I believe that God has placed within every human being at least a measure of an inner "warning system" to protect us from being easily deceived – just as He has given us all a conscience. It is something that He has built into every one of us, in His mercy. (I guess a lot of it is simply 'common sense'). However, Christians should have an even greater advantage in this area, because we have the "inner witness" of the Holy Spirit, and the 'still small voice' of the Lord speaking to us every day.

But what I have found again and again with people who give themselves over to some form of deception is that they often "override" these inner alarms. They go against their 'better judgment'. They ignore the little voice deep inside them that is telling them that there is something wrong. Christians today do this all the time. That is how they get themselves involved in such foolish deceptions.

This may all sound very obvious, but I am telling you this one basic thing alone could wipe out half the deception in the church right now. If only people would listen to these internal 'alarm bells' and act with common sense, half of it would be gone overnight.

The Bible is very clear that the Last Days are a time of such widespread deception that it would "deceive if possible the very elect". It also shows that much of this deception will arise from WITHIN the church – luring believers who have "itching ears". Do we see evidence of this kind of thing taking place today? Absolutely! In fact, some of it is at a level that is truly shocking. And yet it is all accepted as perfectly "normal" by many Christians.

One of the problems, of course, is that those who bring in these deceptions are usually 'trusted' by the congregation. They have a reputation and they put across some very convincing-sounding arguments and surround the whole thing with Biblical terminology. And thus the deception is harder to spot. (After all, if it were not "deceptive" then it would not be called 'deception'!) People see spiritual power operating and assume that it "must be God". But this is a very dangerous assumption to make in these days.

As I said in a previous chapter, there is also a lot of "peer pressure" involved as well. For if everyone in the church is getting into something, then shouldn't you just ignore those little 'alarm bells' and jump right in? This is what is happening all the time in the church right now. And some preachers are very good at making people feel that they are 'hindering the Spirit' if they do not get involved.

So how do you avoid being deceived in this way?

Very simply, you do not go along to these meetings in a "gullible" frame of mind. And you do not allow yourself to be carried along with the crowd. You listen carefully to the preaching and make sure that it truly is Biblical. Then you watch the ministry happening down the front of the meeting and discern whether it really is of God or not. You do not "override" any feelings of unease or any 'alarm bells' going off inside you. And you do not allow yourself to be swayed by 'peer pressure'. Even if the whole church is getting into something, it does not mean that you have to. If you do not feel quite "right" about it then DO NOT GET

INVOLVED. If you need to, make some excuse and get out of there! You do not have to get involved in things that do not feel spiritually "right" to you.

A lot of people today will go to the front to get something "imparted" to them by almost every visiting speaker – almost as a matter of course. I tell you, in today's climate this can be a very dangerous thing to do. In fact, some of this 'impartation' business has very flimsy backing in Scripture. Who knows what on earth these preachers are imparting? And who knows where they picked it up? I tell you, deceiving spirits are commonplace today, and I believe they are being imparted to Christians on a large scale.

Let me give you an example. I received the following account from a preacher in England not too long ago:

"There were about 20 fellow ministers all gathered together in one large room at a local minister's house. We were introduced to the special guest... The next 3 hours were the weirdest three hours I have ever had to endure. We started listening to [her] testimony which seemed very powerful, next she spoke of the times that she meets with the Angel Gabriel and other spiritual beings, next we moved on to portals between this world and the next and then finally to how she was going to open up a portal to Heaven in the room that we were all in. Now things started to happen, really crazy things and strange noises... As [she] moved around the room ministering to individual people they were crashing to the ground, bouncing up and down, running around as if on fire and making all sorts of sounds. When she came to me she had no prophetic words for me and nothing happened to me so she just moved on. My Vineyard friend was the first to crash to the floor. Since that day his church has taken on a different guise, it is not the same church any more."

Now, you should know that this 'guest speaker' is a woman who is quite high up in the Prophetic Movement – well known and highly regarded (except by people with discernment). This is typical of the kind of thing that happens in a lot of the more "powerful" prophetic meetings today. People are so desperate for a 'touch' or a spiritual experience that they will fall for anything. I myself have been in one of her meetings and what I saw was people making involuntary "bat"-like movements all over the building and an eerie 'wailing' noise filling the air. It was truly awful.

Now, it should not surprise us that there are strong deceptions or "powerful delusions" around today, for this is exactly what the Scriptures predict will happen. All the way through the New Testament we are warned of these days – over and over again.

However, one of the problems we have is that God actually does 'strange and unusual' things Himself (especially in Revivals). So we cannot simply throw out everything unusual. Just think about the Book of Acts for a moment. Not only are there healings and miracles and demons being cast out right through the whole book, but there are also occasionally angels appearing with instructions from the Lord, and an abundance of dreams, visions and prophecies, etc. So we see that God is definitely a SUPERNATURAL GOD. He does "unusual" things. Angelic visitations DO HAPPEN. Prophetic signs DO OCCUR. But please notice that all of these things have a certain holy "character" about them. And that is the key right there. They have a holy character, because they come from a holy God.

Being a strong Pentecostal-type Christian myself, I expect to see believers speaking in tongues and moving in the gifts of the Holy Spirit – just like in the New Testament. But as I stated earlier, God never goes against His own holy character, or against Scripture. And as I often say, we may see Him do 'unusual' things but I believe we need to draw the line at "weird" or ugly. Some of the deception that is around right now has a 'touchy-feely' New Age sense about it. Remember that the New Age movement majors on "inner healing" and unusual spiritual experiences. I do not believe in 'guided visualization' or anything of that kind. And neither am I very fond of the writings of Catholic mystics or the like.

However, I have personally found it very helpful to immerse myself in the writings of past Revivalists and the accounts of great moves of God. A lot of the men and women involved in these

Revivals lived very close to God and knew Him intimately. They knew His holiness, they knew His glory, and they knew His love. And it is enormously helpful to one's discernment to immerse oneself in these writings, I have found. I would recommend this to all Christians everywhere.

If you have been touched or involved in any way with manifestations or experiences that you think may not have been from God, then I urge you to utterly RENOUNCE (with your mouth, but also from the depths of your very being in Jesus' name) any links or involvement with that experience or 'anointing'. Please do not put this off, my friends. Some of this stuff is extremely dangerous. RENOUNCE it today.

"ROMANCING JESUS" – ANOTHER DISTORTION

While we are on this subject, I must mention another teaching that has widely infiltrated the Prophetic movement and also large sections of the modern Prayer movement today (including IHOP, the Call and related groups). When I lived in Kansas City I got a close-up view of all this, because Kansas City is a major center for the spread of this teaching around the world.

(It is interesting to note that Todd Bentley himself was involved with IHOP, and even had an office there at one stage).

So what does this "Romancing Jesus" teaching involve? Well, it uses the concept that the church is the "Bride of Christ" – but instead of simply applying this to the WHOLE church – the 'corporate' body – it tries to apply it to individual Christians (even MEN), turning them into lovers or little 'brides' of Jesus (so to speak). Often King Solomon's love poetry from the Song of Solomon is used, and people are taught to approach God more-or-less like a "romantic lover" – as He woos and romantically pursues them with an 'inflamed heart'. Old Christian mystics and the like are often quoted in support of all this. In most places there are attempts made to bring some balance to the teaching, but even in its mildest form I believe it creates dangerous distortions in people's understanding of WHO GOD IS and how we are to approach Him. This teaching is increasingly popular – and is spreading at a rapid rate. And some people are certainly taking it to an extreme. Below are several emails I received from readers, commenting on what they had seen regarding this teaching:

"D--" writes:

I ran into this a few weeks ago at our home fellowship. A woman whom I see to be very Spirit filled, was talking to us at the dinner table about being taken into the "upper chambers" where Jesus laid her down on a bed of roses (because He is the Rose of Sharon He can do that, she said), and that He made love to her. She described to me this whole scene as if it were out of a romance novel. The thought of Jesus actually making love to me made me sick... I was actually disheartened, grieved and shocked that she was talking about this. What gets me is that her friends who were with her all agreed as if this was sound biblical doctrine.

"J----" writes:

I just went to a ladies retreat two weeks ago and the theme was this same "lover Jesus" as portrayed in a book they used called, "With an Everlasting Love"... It was so godless and selfish and full of "eros", putting thoughts and feelings in whoever reads it that certainly did not bring glory to God... I now have the opportunity to confront the pastor's wife about this teaching that literally every woman fell for (except me!) and was "wooed" by their sensuality as women and the need for love, that they sucked it right up.

"R---" writes:

I moved here to KC 2 years ago to attend IHOP.... I have been so confused by the whole up-sweep of the "Bridal Paradigm" and ravished heart of Jesus and Song of Solomon. I cannot relate to Jesus as romantic lover, nor do I want to!! I am trying to have clean thoughts and a pure heart. I want a Godly husband to be that for me, to model Christ's love and headship. All my friends tell me,

"Jesus is your husband - let Him be your first love and your provider". As if I should shun men and give up on the idea of marriage.

The Editor of a Prophetic Newsletter - who follows the whole movement closely – writes:

I too have been concerned about this for a while. In particular I have seen much written about intimacy without any reference to obeying the revealed will of God. Jesus said, "If you love me, you will obey my commands." The intimacy emphasis is not just out of balance, it is dangerously soulish, promising emotional experiences and opening up the way to deceiving spirits if pursued too far.

"C---" writes:

What's amazing is how the presence of this teaching is like yeast. For a few years I was among believers who had absorbed 'bridal paradigm' teaching out of KC. It had a weird way of rubbing off. Even though I'd never even encountered it myself directly, for awhile I'd unwittingly absorbed some of it & had some dreams I now know came from unclean spirits. Thankfully my discernment antennaes began picking up on & rejecting the unholy nature of all this. Like many such excesses, it's the mixture that results when deception is mingled with the pure revelation of the Spirit that's so very, very deadly.

"L---" writes:

There is a strange message behind this Bridal Paradigm. -It was shown at the CALL in Kansas City. I was there. I witnessed this. There was a call to all those young people who were in attendance at this KC gathering and a few older - to pledge a marriage covenant right then that night to be MARRIED to Christ.

There was a Marriage Canopy held up for a marriage procession as hundreds marched under it as to become covenantly married to Christ. They made it seem so righteous and holy - So - many threw away their discernment and followed the leaders - forgetting that the marriage actually takes place in heaven at the marriage supper of the Lamb.

CBN NEWS REPORT – JAN 6, 2002:

"THE CALL" IN KANSAS CITY: A Marriage Covenant with Jesus. By Wendy Griffith, CBN News Reporter, CBN.com.

Some 20,000 mostly young people packed the Kansas City Convention Center on New Year's Eve for a wedding ceremony unlike any other... as each person who came embarked on a marriage covenant with the Bridegroom of Heaven... From noon until midnight they danced and sang, fasted and prayed, and got ready to get married to Jesus.

"There's going to be a wedding and God is raising up friends of the Bridegroom to prepare the church, there's going to be a wedding!"

One by one, thousands of men and women, young and old, made their vows and walked under the prayer shawl symbolizing their commitment to Jesus....

Stewart Greaves, a 30-year-old, said, "I really feel like the Lord is calling young people to fall madly in love with Him. I've always felt that the difference between religion and relationship is intimacy with Jesus..."

Here in Kansas City, there has already been a tremendous focus on the bridal love of Jesus... where for three and a half years, a team of prophetic singers, intercessors and others have held 24-hour-a-day praise and worship focusing on Jesus as the bridegroom.

FROM a BOOK that has been Required Reading at this IHOP School of Ministry in Kansas City:

"He [God] has given Himself to both the exhilarations and the

woundings of a lovesick heart. When He gazes upon me, He sees through the eyes of love and desire. He comes before me and says, 'I am a Man in love. I am a God that burns with desire, and I have set My affections on you. I am an all-consuming fire of love, and you are the inheritance that My Father has promised me. Will you receive My love?'" (Pg 57).

"O Gaze Eternal,
How penetrating are Your Fires
Rushing through my darkest places
With the burning streams of Desire
Leaving me naked, purged and bare
... Yet embraced...
You take hold of my weakest places
And kiss them with Your mercy
Lifting up my low grounds
With your mighty love so holy..." (Pg 52).

"She lifted her arms wide to the Lord and said with all of her strength and her love, 'Enjoy me. Right here, right now, in my absolute weakness, enjoy me.'" (Pg 84).

NOTE: The above book, which is entitled, "Deep Unto Deep – The Journey of the Embrace", goes on and on in a similar vein for 200 pages. We remind you again that this is an officially recommended publication at this Kansas City prayer center, with a foreword by the leader of the movement Mike Bickle himself. It has been "Required Reading" for the young people at their Ministry School.

(There are a number of books by IHOP founder Mike Bickle on this topic as well – such as "Passion For Jesus" and 'The Pleasures of Loving God'. I find them pretty distasteful but not nearly as bad as the book quoted above).

A NEW 'PARADIGM'

You will notice in the above quotes that the term "Bridal

Paradigm" is used. This is the semi-official label for this teaching. So what exactly does it mean? Well, a 'paradigm' is a new mindset or "world-view". It seems that through this teaching these people are now viewing Jesus and Christianity through an entirely new set of lenses, so to speak – i.e., through this 'Bridal' Paradigm. For many, this now seems to be their dominant understanding of how we should approach God.

When you hear people using such terms as "passion for Jesus", the "ravished" heart of God, 'lovesick', swooning, inflamed, 'fascinated', etc, you know that you are around people who are influenced by this teaching. And when you hear Christian songs that say, "I kiss you with the kisses of my mouth" or "Take me into your inner chamber", etc, you know where that song-writer is getting his or her inspiration. Some of this is quite subtle, and is spreading unnoticed through large sections of the body of Christ in a somewhat 'mild' form. I guess on that level it may be fairly harmless, but what concerns me are the large numbers of young people who are being exposed to the full-on "Bridal Paradigm" teaching without realizing what a dangerous distortion of Scripture it really is – and how harmful. Imagine the effect on young MALES when they are told to act like a 'bride' towards Jesus – another male! I'm sure you can see how quickly this degenerates into a view of God that is completely unscriptural and unhealthy.

The fact is our understanding of "WHO GOD IS" is crucially important. It is the one thing that shapes so much of our faith and our relationship with the Lord. At the heart of a lot of cults and deceptions is a fundamental misapprehension of the true character and nature of God – i.e., "Who He is – How we approach Him". It really does affect EVERYTHING.

As history shows us again and again, to the equal degree that we lose our grasp of the real character and nature of God – to this same degree we will lose genuine Christianity. And sadly that is exactly what this 'Bridal' teaching is doing: It is distorting our very understanding of God's nature and character. In fact, when you look at a lot of the teachings that have come out of the

"Prophetic/Toronto/River" circles in recent years this is precisely what many of them do. It is almost as if they believe in a slightly "different God". They seem to believe in a God who constantly does weird or ugly or bizarre things – explaining that "God offends the mind to reveal the heart." And they seem to believe in a God who actually enjoys it when we approach Him like some sensuous "lover" with spiritual 'romance' on our mind. I don't know what kind of God they are talking about, but it is not the God of the Bible. And that is really the crux of the matter right there. Our understanding of "WHO GOD IS" fundamentally affects EVERYTHING about the way we worship Him, the way we pray to Him, and the things we think are "acceptable" in His sight.

I'm sure you can see why, at the end of the day, a lot of the issues I have with the Prophetic movement boil down to this one thing: Their understanding of 'WHO GOD IS' and how we are to approach Him. That is really at the root of all our differences.

My own views are shaped by – amongst other things – years of studying the way God has ACTED in His dealings with men down the centuries. Of course, Scripture is the most important source for this, but we also see the same thing in every great move of God down through history as well. What do these show us? They show us God's character – how He ACTED again and again – and the things that are of crucial importance to Him. In the Bible we see God DESCRIBING Himself through His apostles and prophets – and through His own holy son. We see the SAME GOD who has NEVER CHANGED – from ancient history until now. And I'm sorry, but I simply do not see the "fruit-cake" God that these people see. And I have to believe that this is one huge reason why they are so prone to deception.

So how do we know, at the most fundamental level, what God's character is like and what His most dominant attributes are? Well, we certainly know that He is a God of love and mercy and grace. We also know that He is a God of justice and judgment – a God of vengeance who will by no means acquit the guilty. But what is the single thing that most represents His character? What is His single most predominant attribute?

It is quite simple to answer this question, for God answers it Himself in Scripture. His single most overriding attribute is "HOLINESS". The Bible makes this very clear. How? By showing us inside the very throneroom of God – and by telling us the one characteristic of God that is repeated over and over in His presence, day and night, throughout all eternity. The prophet Isaiah tells us exactly what this is: "I saw also the Lord sitting upon a throne, high and lifted up, and his train filled the temple... And one cried to another and said, holy, holy, holy is the LORD of hosts: The whole earth is full of his glory. And the posts of the door moved at the voice of him that cried, and the house was filled with smoke" (Is 6:1-5, KJV). Throughout the whole Bible we are never told of any other characteristic of God that is repeated over and over in His presence in this way.

And the same throneroom scene that Isaiah saw is described again in Revelation chapter 4 – where we are told that the four beasts cry, "Holy, holy, holy" day and night without ceasing, and the 24 elders cast down their crowns before God's throne – over and over again. It is "HOLINESS" that is the chief characteristic of God! Never is any other attribute repeated three times together for such maximum emphasis. This is the only one – "HOLY, HOLY, HOLY." And we are also told that, "without holiness, no man shall see the Lord." (Heb 12:14).

It is interesting to note that the full title of the book of Revelation is the "Revelation of Jesus Christ". So in many ways it is a book that 'reveals' who Jesus is and what He is really like. And when John (the 'beloved' disciple) first sees the glorified Christ in Revelation 1, we are told that such is His terror-inducing holiness and glory that John fell at his feet "as though dead." This is the true Jesus – as He really is.

In every true Revival, it is this God of majesty who reveals himself. For Revival is the Glory of God coming down. It is His very throneroom presence coming down amongst men. Thus, even His own children should approach Him with awe. And if we do not pray to this God, then we should not expect Revival at all. That is one of the basic lessons of Revival history. We must pray to the 'RIGHT GOD' if we are going to see true Revival.

As a student of Revival I can tell you that the old Revivalists prayed to a God who is very different from what is being presented today. And their understanding of "WHO GOD IS" was utterly crucial to their obtaining Revival. They prayed to a God of holiness and majesty and awe – a God of glory who hates sin, yet sent His son to die for sinners. And we had better learn to pray to this same holy God if we are to expect Revival in our own day.

TRUE "INTIMACY" WITH GOD

A lot is spoken today about having 'intimacy' with Jesus. And I agree with this. To know Him deeply is very important. But how exactly do we come to know Him in a much deeper way?

Well, in my experience, unless there is a focus on God's HOLINESS, then we have little hope of coming to know Him intimately at all. We have just seen that Holiness is by far God's most overriding characteristic. I want to put it to you, that unless you come to know the depths of His Holiness, then your intimacy with Him will be very limited. This is the dominant attribute of God.

When I was 17 years old I got filled with the Holy Spirit and underwent a kind-of "mini-Revival" in my life. I began to read Revival books, and noticed that Holiness was a major theme of most Revivals down the ages. And so, just like in the books, I began to "agonize" in prayer before a holy God. And I began to sense a massive "breaking through" into His presence in prayer. Many times I found myself (as it were) in the very 'throneroom' presence of God, where all I could do was behold His glory and majesty in awe – often with tears streaming down my face. "HOLY HOLY HOLY". Sometimes I have been unable to speak or utter any word for hours at a time – because no words are sufficient. This is the God that I came to deeply love. A 'HOLY' God. And I believe that knowing God deeply in this way is for every believer.

The pathway into a deeper experience of God's LOVE is the pathway of HOLINESS. We must have "clean hands and a pure heart". And we must come to see how utterly Holy our God is – Holy beyond words and almost beyond comprehension. The more we get a grasp of God's HOLINESS, the more we ourselves desire holiness, and the closer and closer to Him we become. I have seen this and I know it is true.

Which is why I have such a problem with the "Jesus as Lover" teaching. Because it brings God down to "our level" – a sentimental romantic level rather than a 'throneroom' one. It paints God, not as Holy, but as excessively 'emotional', as He woos and romantically pursues us with His "inflamed" heart. It is an awful distortion. I believe it actually ruins a lot of people's relationship with God – rather than helping it. In many ways it is a "false Jesus" that is being preached – and the approach is completely wrong.

However, one thing that could be seen as "good" in the prayer movements that embrace this teaching is their emphasis on fasting and prayer. And certainly I am all for that! We need more prayer and fasting in this world, not less! But one thing that needs to be watched in some of these groups is what they call a 'Bridegroom Fast'. At times this is not just simply fasting and praying for Revival or for more of God's presence, but rather it can have a whole different meaning. As one observer commented: *"I have had experience with some ministry that included what they call a "bridegroom fast" where they mourn in "lovesickness" for the purpose of experiencing more of divine Love. Seems to be really over-emphasizing emotional experiences."* And thus their prayer and fasting is sometimes not what it seems – and I would strongly caution people to watch for this.

In summarizing this section, I just want to reiterate that one of the most important keys to discernment in these days is to KNOW YOUR HOLY GOD – and to know Him INTIMATELY. All

Scripture and Revival history point to the fact that it is the "throneroom" God – the God of all glory – that we must get to know if we are to come into the deepest heart communion and intimacy with Him. The 'Fear' of the Lord really is the beginning of wisdom. We need to seek and seek and SEEK this wonderfully Holy God with all our hearts.

CHAPTER SIX

WANTED - REAL PROPHETS!

*"May the Lord send us prophets – terrible men, who cry aloud
and spare not, who sprinkle nations with unctionized woes –
men too hot to hold, too hard to be heard, too merciless to spare."*
-Leonard Ravenhill.

As I spoke about in the first chapter, even many years before I left
the Prophetic movement I was coming to believe more and more
that the whole movement was failing God. And it was not just the
"manifestations" that convinced me of this. It was the lack of any
real prophetic "trumpet call" to the church. As I wrote in one of my
most outspoken articles on this subject:

*The history of the Prophetic - just like other movements that have
gone before - is a history of compromise. Too many prophets have
made themselves thoroughly comfortable with the present system.
They know that if they keep their mouth shut in certain areas and
"emphasize the positive" (as the old advertising slogan goes) then
they can do quite nicely for themselves without too much risk.
Thus, through their silence they have become nodding supporters
of the status quo. They are Laodicean prophets in a Laodicean
age...*

*Speaking specifically about the Laodicean church, Jesus said: "As
many as I love I REBUKE AND CHASTEN: Be zealous therefore
and REPENT" (Rev 3:19). Because He loves His church, Jesus
seeks to warn and rebuke her before it is too late. It is totally*

obvious what message a prophet must bring in a lukewarm age. It is right there in black and white. "REBUKE AND CHASTEN" - a call to large-scale REPENTANCE. Prophets have always been appointed to be God's mouthpiece - to represent His heart. And there is simply no doubt what they should be doing in any "Laodicean" situation. Today's prophets are utterly failing God in this regard...

What we have now is a Prophetic movement that can live quite happily with the status quo - side by side with a thoroughly lukewarm church. We hold our conferences and give our positive and glowing messages of the "great days ahead" with barely a hint of "rebuking and chastening". After all, we wouldn't want to 'offend' anyone, would we?

The movement that was supposed to be a THREAT to compromise and lukewarmness - and its leaders - has now become compromised and lukewarm itself...

There is all this talk about "coming Elijahs" today. I tell you, if Elijah did arrive in the church, most of these people would not know where to hide themselves fast enough. Do you think he would stand for the nonsense that we call "charismatic church meetings" today?

The time has come for TRULY RADICAL prophets of God to arise. The hour is late and the time for measured and mild words is at an end. Prophets, let the fire of God consume you, and come forth bearing words that will SHAKE THE CHURCH. Nothing less will do. A tepid and insipid Prophetic? -AWAY WITH IT FOREVER.

WHERE DID THE ROT BEGIN?

God once gave me an analogy that the TRUE Prophetic is like a three-legged stool – but that today's Prophetic movement has focused overwhelmingly on just two of the legs. (Thus the whole thing is falling over). The two legs that have been focused-on are Revelatory Experiences and Personal Prophecy. (These are the legs that are popular and have that "wow" factor). The leg that has been neglected is the great "anchor" leg of Repentance – which has always played a major role in all true Prophetic ministry down the ages.

In other words, the modern Prophetic became prone to compromise and deception because it majored on the popular, crowd-pleasing aspects and neglected the "hard words" – the rebuking and chastening that today's Lukewarm church so desperately needs to hear.

There are a lot of ministries out there today majoring on 'words of knowledge'. They can go down a whole line of people "wowing" them with personal prophecy. But this is hardly the piercing repentance that the church desperately needs, is it?

And there are many ministries today that major on prophetic revelation. They can share all kinds of visions, words, revelatory experiences, etc. But again, where is the piercing repentance preaching of old?

I have been forced to conclude that there is a Prophetic movement in the world today that is very far removed from the word 'Prophet'. It sells truckloads of books and holds untold conferences, but at the end of the day it is a mealy-mouthed travesty of the word 'Prophetic'. It retains its popularity because it is almost always "positive" and uplifting. The voice of an Amos or Jeremiah is rarely (if ever) heard in its ranks – let alone a "John the Baptist". It is almost never blunt or confrontational – especially about sin in the church.

Isn't it true that the Prophetic has become little more than a circus today? People come to have their ears tickled – to be titillated rather than convicted. And they will pay good money for it. "For so did their fathers to the false prophets" (Lk 6:26, KJV). Don't you think that God will bring judgment upon "prophets" who deliver ear-tickling words to a Laodicean church? Isn't this the very opposite of what they need?

Ever so conveniently, today's prophets seem to have abandoned the "unpopular" side of their mandate, preferring the acclaim and popularity of thrilling crowds with visions and revelations of the "great things God is about to do", etc. Thus the people constantly flock to hear "some new thing" just as they did with the false prophets of old.

It is little wonder to me that today's Prophetic movement has become renowned amongst many evangelicals as one of the "flakiest" movements the church has ever seen. They take one look at the whole scene and conclude that something is very wrong. And sadly, they are absolutely right.

All the way through history it was always the FALSE PROPHETS who told of the "great things" that were just around the corner. They were always popular with the crowds. Meanwhile the true prophets were often reviled and persecuted because they brought an uncompromising message of SHAKING, CHANGE and REPENTANCE. And this is the exact message that today's church most needs to hear.

A TRUE PROPHETIC

As I said, there seems to have been a great attempt to remove the "prophet" from Prophetic today. It is high time we put it back. What is desperately needed in this hour are John-the-Baptists to bring the most piercing cry that this church has ever heard. Nothing less will do. The church must be shaken and changed. And God surely does want a "Prophetic" movement to do exactly that. (Just perhaps not the one we see around us today). For if He can find no prophets doing their job, how can the church ever come into true Revival?

As A.G. Gardiner declared, "When a prophet is accepted and

deified, his message is lost. The prophet is only useful so long as he is stoned as a public nuisance calling us to repentance, disturbing our comfortable routines, breaking our respectable idols, shattering our sacred conventions."

I am convinced that God is about to raise up a company of John-the-Baptists in this hour who will refuse to compromise His word. Many have been waiting for years in the wilderness for this time. For it is in the desert place that God deals once and for all with the 'fear of man'. Soon they will arise, as if from nowhere, to speak a piercing word and to restore all that is lost. These men and women will want no part of the "prophetic circus" that we see around us today. They will be the most 'ordinary' people speaking under the most extraordinary anointing. A humble company – and pure of heart. The John-the-Baptists are coming!

WHAT ARE REAL PROPHETS LIKE?

We are told in Scripture that John the Baptist came "in the spirit and power of Elijah". And I believe there needs to be something of that same spirit upon any prophet who would see the lukewarm church repent in our own day. There was something of a "holy violence" about these ministries – Elijah, Elisha and John the Baptist – that is worth taking note of. By their very nature they were blunt, uncompromising, fearless messengers of God. They attacked the sin and compromise of their day with cutting power, for the full authority of the Living God was behind every word that they spoke. Their words were like a consuming fire, a piercing two-edged sword, a 'hammer that breaks the rock into pieces'. And they stood unbending in the name of truth and of righteousness, to put to flight God's enemies, to rebuke His wayward people, and to again lift up His standard amidst the darkness of their time.

Witness the fearless prophet Elijah on top of Mt Carmel (1 Kings 18). At his word there has not been one drop of rain in Israel for three and a half years. And now here he is, the only man who dares openly oppose the evil Baal-worshipping empire under cruel queen/witch Jezebel. Hear Elijah lay down his mocking challenge to the Baal priests and prophets: "Cry aloud, for he is a god; either he is meditating, or he is busy... Or perhaps he is sleeping and must be awakened" (v27). And then, at the time of the evening sacrifice, we see Elijah, that fearless prophet of God, call fire down from heaven right before the startled eyes of all present. "And when all the people saw it, they fell on their faces: and they said, The LORD, He is the God; the LORD, He is the God. And Elijah said unto them, Take the prophets of Baal; let not one of them escape. And they took them: And Elijah brought them down to the brook Kishon, and slew them there" (v 39-40, KJV).

Now we jump to 2 Kings chapter one. The rebellious and evil king of Samaria has just sent fifty soldiers to bring the prophet Elijah down from the hill on which he sits. "And Elijah answered and said to the captain of fifty, "If I am a man of God, then let fire come down from heaven and consume you and your fifty men". And fire came down from heaven and consumed him and his fifty" (v10). Rather foolishly, the king then sends another fifty soldiers to bring Elijah down. These too are consumed by fire in exactly the same way. (You see, the Elijah ministries carry something of the 'regal dignity' of God. They carry the fullness of the word of the Lord. They are not at the beck and call of any man – not even a king. They stand in a unique place – "The Lord God, before whom I STAND." Their word, their ministry, their comings and goings are at the mercy of no-one but the Lord). And thus, it is not until the next captain of fifty comes to Elijah on his knees, begging and pleading, that he agrees to go down with him to see the king.

The above incidents, which are typical of the kinds of things that took place in the lives of both Elijah and Elisha, demonstrate not only their power and authority under God, but also the spiritually 'violent' nature of this kind of ministry. One Scripture that has been given to myself and others again and again in relation to the coming move of God is Mt 11:12- "... from the days of John the Baptist until now the kingdom of heaven suffers violence, and the violent take it by force." And another key Scripture "judgment begins at the house of God." It is the church that must first repent. God is coming to "clean house" and He will use His true prophets to do it. And woe to all who are found to be false or compromised in that day.

WHERE IS THE BOLDNESS?

One of the things that most grieves me about today's Prophetic is that it does not come across in any way as truly bold or daring or uncompromising. And yet true prophets are SUPPOSED to be bold and outspoken and daring – no question about it. Historically, they are the ones who will make a stand when no-one else will. If you look down the annals of history, that is one of the most obvious hallmarks of a true prophet. As Leonard Ravenhill said, "Mere preachers may help anybody and hurt nobody; but prophets will stir everybody and madden somebody. The preacher may go *with* the crowd; the prophet goes *against* it." I'm sorry, but I simply do not see this kind of uncompromising boldness in today's Prophetic movement at all. They may fondly wish for it, but they certainly do not have it. And to me, this is one of the most glaring lacks of the entire movement.

God spoke to me many years ago about the major qualification required to enter into true Reformation and Revival. He simply said: "WHO DARES WINS". God showed me that it is not "who PROPHESIES wins". (For to merely bring forth 'words' does not necessarily mean that you will enter in). And it is not even "who PRAYS wins" (though prayer is vital, of course). The most critical thing of all is DARING. Because only those who 'dare' can win their way into a truly radical move of God. Ours must be a 'violent' faith – a violent DARING, which takes the kingdom by force. Only then can we enter into true Reformation and Revival.

In Martin Luther's day, many leaders were well aware that some form of Reformation was essential. But they were shocked at the audacity of Luther, who took on the entire Roman Catholic empire and won. For there is a day for RECKLESS DARING, my friends,

AND THAT DAY IS NOW.

It is noticeable at such times that there are many "prudent" souls who counsel caution and gradualism. But the day for such lukewarm 'prudence' must end if we are to take the kingdom. Friends, the days of timidity and hiding our lamp under a bushel are long gone. It is time to shout the truth from the housetops, and it is the church who must hear it first.

"JUDGMENTAL" PROPHECIES

Another thing about today's Prophetic that tends to make it so compromised is its insistence that basically all New Testament prophecy (meaning us today) must be for 'edification, exhortation and comfort'. Many in the Prophetic movement totally believe this, but I must say I have great difficulty with it being applied in such a blanket way. I certainly believe it is true of the level where "all may prophesy" – where encouraging and uplifting the local saints is the main goal (see 1 Cor 14 v 3 & 31). But to apply it across the board, especially to those called to a higher level of prophetic ministry, is unscriptural and terribly damaging in my view.

While I can see that some self-styled "prophets" today get carried away with harsh, judgmental, 'anti-everything' prophecies originating largely out of their own bitterness or rejection, I also see that there is a crying need for true prophets to arise crying "REPENT" in our day, much as the Old Testament prophets did with Israel. In fact, as a student of Revival I would have to say that the vast majority of true Revivalists down through history (Edwards, Whitefield, Finney, Booth, Sung, Goforth, Roberts, etc) have actually carried out this role of an Old Testament-type prophet in their own generation – calling God's people to repentance – or else judgment!

The church today is in the same lukewarm condition that Israel was in when God sent prophets to warn them of the consequences of their sin. Can anyone honestly tell me that He would NOT send similar men and women to warn His people today of the danger they are in? Surely we need an Amos, a Jeremiah, a John-the-Baptist now more than ever – to wake us up!

Do we honestly think that such a man would speak soothing words? No! He would speak words of fire, convicting us of whatever sin could be found in us. Charles Finney and every other Revivalist would roll in their graves to hear of "prophets" who are only allowed to prophesy sweetness and light all the time. And going by the book of Acts, so would the apostle Paul!

For those who say that it is not "New Testament" to prophesy of 'sin, righteousness and judgment' (John 16:8) I would reply that JESUS is our example in the New Testament. And Jesus many times spoke and acted JUST LIKE an Old Testament prophet, the same as John the Baptist did. Jesus was the one who wept over Jerusalem, but who also called the religious leaders "snakes" and hypocrites. "How shall you escape the damnation of hell?" He cried. Jesus delivered the Beatitudes, but he also made a whip and overturned the tables of the moneychangers in the temple, saying "Zeal for my Father's House has consumed me." He told his audience that the blood of all the past holy men would be on the heads of that generation. Does this sound like "only edification, exhortation and comfort" to you? Jesus is our example, and barely ever did he prophesy mere 'sweetness and light'.

If God is truly calling us to bring a 'strong, convicting' word, then let us do it – with no fear. All the true Revivalists did. And let us away with this nonsense about "only encouragement and edification". I frankly cannot stand to hear such unscriptural talk any longer. Perhaps it is true for brand new believers, but not for mature prophetic ministries. Yes, there are harsh, self-appointed 'judges' out there giving prophecy a bad name. But that is not what I am talking about here.

But while we are on that subject, just a word here about the (often young) brash, immature 'prophet'-types who go around "blasting" people with bludgeoning, judgmental prophecies, etc. (I used to be one of these myself, in my young days!) Often, such 'prophets' may have a true calling on their life, but their immaturity, their (unknowing) pride and arrogance, and their secret rebellion make them very dangerous to themselves and to others. Until they allow God to bring true brokenness and humility into their lives (an often painful process), then they will usually end up causing more harm than good wherever they go. There is a time for rebuking (though only mature ministries should really consider it), but most of the time there is no substitute for "speaking the truth in love". Wisdom, patience, gentleness, meekness and love should all be part of the strength that God has built into our ministries. Otherwise we can end up doing great damage to His precious sheep. (For words can inflict great harm). Please think and pray about these things, my friends, if you have the tendencies of just such a "lone ranger".

LOVE PEOPLE PLEASE!

A lot of people think that to be a prophet you need to be some kind of "hard" individual. And yes – there is a kind of "toughness" involved – to stand up against the flow. But the fact is, without a soft heart towards God and towards people, every one of us is utterly useless to God. If we "HAVE NOT LOVE" then we are nothing but a resounding gong and a clanging cymbal. And the great Revivalists were very aware of this. They knew the crucial truth of the Scripture, "The LOVE of God is shed abroad in our hearts by the Holy Ghost." They knew that love is a vital sign of the FULLNESS of the Spirit. And without it we have nothing.

Thus we commonly find Charles Finney saying things like: "I preached and poured out my soul and my TEARS together." And in fact, here is how he described one of his most powerful sermons: "It seemed to myself as if I could rain hail and love upon them at the same time; or in other words, that I could rain upon them hail, in love. It seemed as if my love to God, in view of the abuse which they heaped upon him, sharpened up my mind to the most intense agony. I felt like rebuking them with all my heart, and yet with a compassion which they could not mistake. I never knew that they accused me of severity; although I think I never spoke with more severity, perhaps, in my life."

As you may have gathered, when I myself was a young Christian I was a total zealot. There is nothing wrong with that, but sadly I was often a zealot without wisdom – and also WITHOUT LOVE. I cared for "truth" more than I cared for people, and I did not even notice that I was often using Truth as a sword to crush people with, rather than set them free.

A lot of young zealous Christians are like that – but I was particularly bad because I had a 'prophetic'-type personality – very intense, very black and white. I would walk into a room full of Christians and start an argument at the drop of a hat. I was not afraid to "blast" anyone. Truth was king – the most important thing – and that was all I cared about. This was not just an "occasional" problem with me – this was the way I lived and breathed. Total, all-out zealotry.

I do not have this approach to life any more – though I still care deeply about truth (for that is the way God made me). Sometimes I will still debate and argue things with people – though very rarely.

Over the years God did a work in me, as He does in all of us. In fact, to change my hardened heart He had to break me and break me and break me some more. And each time He did so, a little bit of LOVE got in. I'm sure He is still doing so today.

I started to realize that from God's point of view, the most precious thing in all the earth is PEOPLE. We can see this in the most famous verse in the Bible – "For God SO LOVED the world...." There it is – He so loves PEOPLE. He sent His son to die for PEOPLE. That is what it is all about.

In the land of New Zealand where I was brought up there is an old Maori saying, which I have to love – "What is the most important thing in this world?... It is people, it is people, it is people."

And yet to me in those early years, it was not "people" that I deeply cared about at all. The only thing I deeply valued was the 'Truth' that I was trying to put across that day. And so I attacked and spiritually "hacked" at people all day long. I was a walking nightmare.

Do you realize the sheer amount of 'breaking' that has to go on in someone like that – to get them to LOVE? Years and years of awful crushing and brokenness. Because I was SO BAD – seriously – I was a danger to the church and to myself.

If you love your 'Truths' more than you love people, then you are an out-and-out Pharisee. Nothing less. And you will create condemnation and death in people, rather than conviction and life.

But if you can get broken enough to truly love people – and value them more than anything in this earth – and then speak Truth to them out of that place of love – then you will become greatly effective. It is all about becoming broken and learning to love others from the heart. If you ask Him to, God will do "whatever it takes" to get you to that place.

This is not to say that you will never speak direct or piercing words. You will – but the whole motivation will be different. In fact, EVERYTHING will be different. You may be very confronting, and speak very direct truths – but it will be in the right spirit. And this God can greatly anoint.

Listen, friends, you can do anything with Truth. You can use it to beat people up or set them free. You can use it to become the most "negative" person on the planet, or you can allow it to break your heart and make you a closer follower of Jesus. You can use it in love, or you can use it in zealous self-righteousness to hammer and condemn people. It is up to you – and the true state of your heart.

All I can pray is that those reading this will stop and consider for a moment. Don't be like me, and take years to discover these most basic things.

Let me ask you a simple question – Do you truly LOVE PEOPLE

more than the 'Truths' you are trying to make them listen to? Do you value them as God does – and realize that He sees them as the most precious thing in all the earth? (Especially His children).

How deeply can we come to realize this truth – that GOD LOVES PEOPLE. Yes – repeat it – "GOD LOVES PEOPLE". And so must we, if we are to represent Him on this planet.

However, in concluding this section, it is important for me to repeat again that I believe there is an hour coming when God's true prophets will arise in this generation – and then look out! Trained for years in the desert for this time, and with hearts overflowing with the love of God, these ministries will preach a heart-piercing message of conviction and fire, awakening and transforming multitudes. The days of a searing John-the-Baptist-type Prophetic must return. Otherwise, what hope for Revival?

"RECEIVING" A PROPHET

It is interesting to note that throughout Scripture there is a tremendous blessing attached to "receiving" a true prophet and his message. Likewise, there is a real curse attached when we reject the one whom the Lord sends. We see this on both a small scale and a large scale, right through the Bible.

This concept of "receiving" a prophet was so important to Jesus that He said: "He who receives a prophet in the name of a prophet shall receive a prophet's reward" (Mt 10:41). He told his disciples that when they came into a new town, "whoever will not receive you nor hear you, when you depart from there, shake off the dust under your feet as a testimony against them. Assuredly, I say to you, it will be more tolerable for Sodom and Gomorrah in the day of judgment than for that city!" (Mk 6:11).

To Jesus it was a very serious thing that Jerusalem and Israel were not only rejecting Him and His message, but also the "prophets and wise men" that He would send to them. The mistreatment of these messengers was in itself a cause for the most severe judgment. If you read the entire passage of Jesus' outcry over Jerusalem in Matt 23:34-39, you can clearly see that this was a major reason for the judgment that was about to come upon them. And indeed, less than forty years later in AD 70, Jerusalem was surrounded by armies and utterly destroyed – just as Jesus had prophesied. It is estimated that over one million Jews were put to death, and the historian Josephus records that so much blood was flowing in the streets at times that it was putting out the fires.

Jesus ends this passage in Matt 23 with a very significant statement: "You shall see Me no more till you say, 'Blessed is He who comes in the name of the Lord!'" Again, this is all about 'welcoming' those whom God sends, rather than rejecting them. Jesus is saying here that He will not come to this people again until they are welcoming of Him and His true messengers. And the same applies to us today.

One of the major questions that arises about America in our day is whether or not she is willing to "receive" the true prophets that God sends to her, like in times past. For prophets are "difficult" people. They always come with an uncomfortable message, and they are not easy to hear or receive. There is always a cost to welcoming a true messenger of God. But has America now grown too comfortable to receive such ones? Has she become too used to having her ears tickled? Is she now so sated with soft words and gentle speeches, with mass entertainment and selfish pleasures, that she will no longer hear the ones who cry "Repent"? If so, then judgment is at the doors. This is one of the greatest fears I have for America today - that she will not receive a true prophet – only one who is false and tickles her ears.

CHAPTER SEVEN

NEEDED: A GREAT REFORMATION!

*"I consider that the chief dangers which will
confront the twentieth century will be:
Religion without the Holy Spirit; Christianity without Christ;
Forgiveness without regeneration; Morality without God
and Heaven without Hell." - William Booth.*

We have all heard of the "State of the nation" addresses that presidents give – but I believe that what we Christians need urgently today is an honest and unflinching assessment of the "state of the church" – especially in the West. The fact is, things are bad and growing demonstrably worse.

For some time now, numerous Christian leaders have candidly admitted that we live in the age of the lukewarm or 'Laodicean' church. But it appears that little if anything is actually being DONE about it.

This is totally unacceptable, because in the book of Revelation (Rev 3:14-22), Jesus makes the following "promise" to the Laodicean church: "So then because you are lukewarm, and neither cold nor hot, I WILL SPEW YOU OUT OF MY MOUTH... Be zealous therefore, and repent" (KJV). Please remember that this is a PROMISE of God. It is not an idle threat. Unless there is swift and deep repentance, then God "promises" to spew the lukewarm church from His mouth.

It is my belief that the role of a prophet is to be a kind of watchman on the walls, to loudly warn those who sleep of approaching danger. In the current situation, there can be little doubt that a prophet's job would be to 'sound the alarm in Zion' – to loudly warn the people until they are awakened to the very real risk of imminent judgment. There is an old saying: "People will not flee danger until they see it". And that is exactly the kind of wake-up call that the church needs right now. She desperately needs to be made to "see" her danger.

Some years ago I made a study of the difference between the New Testament Church as described in the book of Acts, and today's church. I was alarmed to find that in nearly every respect, today's Christianity is so different from that of the Bible as to beggar belief. In New Testament times the Church was like a 'consuming fire' that swept over the whole world, "destroying the works of the devil". Led by fiery, anointed men of God, the early believers constituted a bold, militant, uncompromising force, dedicated to pulling down the devil's strongholds wherever they could be found. These were the 'ground assault' troops of the Most High. They endured much suffering, hardship and persecution in order to see the gospel preached "in all the earth" in their day.

Today, however, we seemingly prefer to set sail for the kingdom of heaven with a little more "style". We are told in the Bible that in the last days, men will be "lovers of pleasures rather than lovers of God". We are also told that, "the time will come when they will not endure sound doctrine; but after their own lusts shall heap to themselves teachers, having itching ears" (2 Tim 4:3, KJV). Isn't it true that we modern believers have invented for ourselves a kind of instant, convenient, 'fast-food' Christianity? A Christianity where all too often the preachers feel it is their role to entertain and cajole, rather than to convict and awaken? A Christianity where for many years now, seeking after "blessings" has seemingly replaced hungering and thirsting after God? A Christianity that is seemingly more concerned with "happiness" than real holiness? Who could deny that this century finds itself home to what is probably the most comfortable, the most materialistic, the most 'fat' and well-fed church in recorded history?

Jesus reported the cry of the Laodicean church as being: "I am rich and increased with goods, and have need of NOTHING" (Rev 3:17, KJV). Incredibly, as we see from this statement, the Laodicean church does not even RECOGNIZE her own appalling spiritual nakedness and bankruptcy! She honestly believes that "all is well"! Certainly, no-one could imagine an era when the church has had so many 'toys', both physical and spiritual. "Rich and increased with goods" we most certainly are in these materialistic days: Lavish church buildings, costly radio and TV programs, bookshops crammed with every conceivable teaching aid and religious gift, expensive conferences and seminars supplying yet more ear-tickling teaching to those with enough dollars to attend. Who could deny that Christianity is 'big business' these days?

J. Lee Grady, the editor of Charisma magazine, commented not long ago: "Just when I thought we charismatics had finally taken enough abuse from the egomaniac ministers in our midst, I've learned that some of our leaders are taking things to a new extreme. We've moved beyond the red carpets, limousines and entourages of the 1990s. A new strain of the celebrity virus is spreading in large segments of the church... One friend of mine in Texas recently inquired to see if a prominent preacher could speak at her conference. The minister's assistant faxed back a list of requirements that had to be met in order to book a speaking engagement. The demands included: (a).. a five-figure honorarium; (b).. a $10,000 gasoline deposit for the private plane; (c).. a manicurist and hairstylist for the speaker; (d).. a suite in a five-star hotel; (e).. a luxury car from the airport to the hotel (2004 model or newer); (f).. room-temperature Perrier... This really makes me wonder how the apostle Paul, Timothy or Priscilla managed ministering to so many people in Ephesus, Corinth and Thessalonica. How did they survive without a manicurist if they broke a nail while laying hands on the sick?"

Mr. Grady had also published another comment about a year earlier, concerning very similar issues: "A widely traveled minister recently gave a message about what he called "the Boaz anointing" at a prominent church in Florida. He then invited anyone who wanted this "new" blessing to come to the altar, where gullible souls were encouraged to deposit a check for $1,500 in the basket. Apparently the Boaz anointing can be yours if you can afford this hefty price. At another church in my city of Orlando, a self-proclaimed prophet said that he would have a personal word of blessing to pronounce over any person who could give $1,000 in the offering. That's right – he was selling personal prophecies. Those who actually gave the amount (yes, some people actually fell for this charlatan) stood up to receive "words.".... I want to rip my shirt in half and throw dust on my head. Why should we be surprised that the church in America is making such a weak impact on society when we are allowing greedy impostors to pollute our pulpits?"

However, lest we kid ourselves that most of these problems are only caused by corrupt or compromised leaders, it would be good to remind ourselves of the old adage that, "The people usually get the leaders they deserve." The fact is, the church has begotten money-hungry charlatans because it rewards and honors and sustains them. A people that live for mammon and pleasure will gather to themselves preachers that have exactly those self-same attributes. Remember, Paul said, "They will HEAP TO THEMSELVES teachers, having itching ears." And this is exactly what we are seeing. Leadership is an enormous problem - but the people are aiding and abetting it.

The Scriptures clearly tell us: "Do not love the world or the things in the world. If anyone loves the world, THE LOVE OF THE FATHER IS NOT IN HIM" (1 Jn 3:15). But who could deny that many Christians today are seemingly more devoted to their career (or to their possessions, or their television) than they are to God? Jesus clearly stated, "You cannot serve God and mammon", yet how many Christians today expend all their energy trying to keep both camps happy? The Bible tells us, "Be not conformed to this world", yet how many Christians today have lifestyles, ambitions and possessions that are literally identical to those of the covetous, materialistic world all around them?

"This was the iniquity of your sister Sodom:" says the Scripture, "She and her daughter had pride, fullness of food, and abundance of idleness; neither did she strengthen the hand of the poor and needy. And they were haughty and committed abomination before Me; therefore I took them away as I saw fit" (Ez 16:49-50).

Where are the prophets who will stand up and cry aloud at these abominations today? Where are the servants of God who will risk everything – their reputation, their ministry, even their very lives – to call a halt to the corruption, the cancer, the all-pervading sickness that is spreading through the camp?

JUDGMENT UPON LEADERS

We noted earlier that the people in the pews are almost as much at fault as their leaders in allowing things to become as sick as they have now become. However, it is very important to note that when the people of Israel fell into a state of serious spiritual decline, God often held the kings and spiritual shepherds of Israel directly responsible. Often, the judgment that fell upon the leaders at such times was far harsher than that which fell upon the nation as a whole. This is because they were some of the few who could have made a real difference. We see this principle at work right down through the Old and New Testaments. And thus Jesus spoke essentially the same message to the religious leaders of His day, as had been spoken to the disobedient king Saul: "The kingdom shall be taken from you and given to another" (1 Sa 28:17 and Mt 21:43). This is a direct pronouncement of judgment upon compromised leaders.

The obvious and brutal truth is this: It is simply not possible to have a lukewarm church unless the leaders are lukewarm, just as Israel was not able to fall into a state of worldliness or idolatry unless her kings and shepherds were men of compromise. The Bible is very clear that those who are raised up as leaders or teachers amongst God's people will have a "stricter" judgment (James 3:1). And when the time for Reformation comes, God will act to bypass or remove such ones from their place over His people. For God can never live with a Laodicean church.

Many leaders today have surrendered in varying degrees to the 'fear of man'. They are afraid to preach uncompromising truth to their congregations for fear that some will become "offended" (not forgetting who pays their salary!) Instead, it almost seems as if they have adopted the modern marketing creed: "Accentuate the positive and eliminate the negative" (complete with warm homilies and amusing anecdotes, of course). No 'sin, righteousness and judgment' preaching here, thankyou! And of course, no desperately-needed REPENTANCE for the lukewarm church, either.

As history shows, God must very often have entirely new leaders and a new movement to go with His new outpouring. This is what true "Reformation" has always been about. And sadly, whenever God is about to do something completely new, many leaders – feeling threatened or envious – oppose it with every ounce of their being. This has unfortunately always been the way. "The previous move persecutes the new move of God." And I expect this time to be no different.

AMERICA IS A LEADER

The USA is a very blessed nation. She has received more Great Awakenings from God than virtually any other country in history, apart from Israel. Quite simply, she has been one of the most blessed nations that the world has ever seen.

However, as we know, along with this has come a leadership role and a great deal of influence. In fact, it is beyond dispute that America is the leading nation in the earth today. And what I have found is that very few Christians have thought about the CONSEQUENCES of America's spiritual leadership in the world. We have just been discussing the fact that spiritual leaders receive a "stricter judgment" according to Scripture. But what about America's leadership? Well, as long as she uses her spiritual influence for good, it is a great thing. But what if she begins to broadcast all over the world a never-ending stream of depravity and spiritual pollution? Will God's blessing remain upon the land? Will she not receive a 'stricter' judgment?

A lot of people don't seem to realize just how utterly dominant America is in the areas of entertainment, culture, propaganda, media – and the "values" from these things that pervade the whole earth. In fact, America is far stronger in these areas than she is in military might. Her influence pervades every corner of the planet – her TV shows, her movies, her music, her fashions, her satellite broadcasts. Quite simply, America is the "propaganda center" of the earth. And the youth of the entire planet increasingly get their values and their world-view from these things.

If you go to Poland or Hong Kong, Ireland or New Zealand, Israel or Japan – right around the globe you will find American culture everywhere – and usually it is totally dominant. The values of an entire generation are being molded by this media deluge. When I was growing up in New Zealand in the 1970's (way down at the bottom of the world), much of our TV programming was American – just as it is in most of the world today. We would watch the Brady Bunch, the Waltons, Little House on the Prairie, Wonderful World of Disney, etc. Mostly "harmless" stuff. But look at what America is broadcasting to the world now: Sex & the City, Big Brother, Spin City, Desperate Housewives, Paris Hilton, Queer Eye for the Straight Guy, etc. Television for teenagers has simply never been as sick or sin-soaked as it is now. Not to mention that every music video is utterly filled with explicit sexual themes and violence. America, what are you doing to the youth of the earth?

Let me ask you a simple question: What is the major force promoting homosexuality on this planet today? Answer: It is

American television, movies and music. How do they do it? By filling TV shows with subtle propaganda; by making movies like "Brokeback Mountain" and then awarding it with three Academy Awards and sending it around the globe; and by promoting huge 'Gay Pride' events, etc. (Gay marches have now spread worldwide – largely from America). Can anyone tell me what God does to civilizations that celebrate and promote homosexuality in this way, and use their influence to spread it as far as they can?

How is it that with the godly history she has, America has become the center for the promotion of homosexuality, promiscuity, teenage sex, drugs, materialism, relativism and every other sickness, right around the whole earth? How is it that she has become the great corruptor of the youth of the entire planet? How is it that a "Christian" country has basically become the "propaganda arm" of the devil? Why is it that the center of the pornography industry, and almost every other sick thing, is based on American soil? And what can we expect God to do about this, and how soon can we expect Him to do it?

The amazing thing is, almost all of this has taken place within one generation. Fifty years ago, most of it would have been totally undreamt of in America. Tell me, has there ever been any other generation of Americans that killed over 40 million unborn babies in the space of just thirty years – mostly for the sake of CONVENIENCE? And has there ever been any other American generation that celebrated homosexuality and fornication and depravity to the degree that is happening now? Can we go back in history and find any generation that even comes close to being as sin-soaked as this one? And can we find a generation of Americans that spread these things over the whole planet – and made huge financial profits by selling corruption to the youth of all the earth? No – we cannot find such things. Nothing even comes close. This generation is unique in American history. We really have to look in the Bible to find anything like it – in the days of Sodom and Gomorrah and the days of Noah – just before judgment hit. Seriously. The USA has never seen anything like this before.

And it is not only the secular media, either. When I was ministering in Nigeria recently, it did not take me long to see the corrupting influence that US Christian TV is having in many of these developing nations. Basically, there have been huge Revivals taking place in Asia, Africa, and South America in recent years – but sadly as these Revivals occur, American influences start to enter in, and before you know it, full-blown "Prosperity" doctrines have become the order of the day. The US television preachers that are beamed in via satellite are particularly harmful. Their obsession with MONEY, hype, flashy suits, and their "success, health & wealth" gospel – all these are having a terrible effect. In essence, what is happening is that God is bringing Revival, and then these televangelists are corrupting and ruining these precious moves of God with their doctrines. Can you imagine "Prosperity" being preached to poverty-stricken peasants? Can you imagine Third World pastors who live like kings? All this and more is what is taking place all over the world. And again, sadly, the center of all this is America. She has tragically become a broadcaster of ever-greater sickness to the entire earth.

It is very difficult for me to stress strongly enough the grave danger in all of this. Do we not realize that entire cities and empires have been destroyed for the very things that the USA is spreading around the globe right now? Do you think God takes it lightly when his Revivals are being ruined and the youth corrupted worldwide?

One thing should be very clear: God cannot live with a nation that He raised up into prominence, which takes that influence and uses it to corrupt the whole earth. He will have to act. I believe that 9-11 and Hurricane Katrina were God's wake-up call to America. They are signs that He is lifting His hand of protection off the land and that judgment hovers nearby.

God is very serious about cutting off the sickness that is being spread around the earth. He has to stop it. He has to sever it at the root. Never has He allowed such a nation to spread such things for long.

I believe there are only two options for America right now: Revival or Judgment. And it is very possible that the hour is so late that her only chance is Revival in the midst of judgment – an outpouring in the midst of storms the like of which she has never seen.

As I write this, the US stock market and credit markets are still in turmoil due to the ongoing Housing Slump – something we have been warning about since 2006. Is it possible that America needs to suffer a Great Depression, or other calamities, in order for her to be humbled and broken enough to turn back to God? Yes – sadly I believe this to be the case. The stranglehold of materialism and apathy must be broken. The sickness must be stopped.

Please PRAY, my friends! Pray for this once-great nation of America – this ancient "Land of Revivals" – that she might have a one last true Awakening before the end. And above all, pray that in the midst of judgment God might remember mercy.

GETTING THE CHURCH "SAVED"

It is an interesting fact that Charles Finney spent his entire ministry preaching to professing Christians. And yet he was called the greatest 'evangelist'! What he was doing was evangelizing the church people – because he found that most of them were not living in a state of true salvation at all. The church was 'unsaved'! Thus his first calling was to the believers of his day – to see them converted. Just like Jesus and the apostles were called first to the Jews – the 'believers' of their time. Finney found himself preaching piercing salvation messages his whole life in church buildings, Bible Colleges and so-on. The "Christians" must be saved.

Actually, you see this pattern in most Revivals down the centuries. In many cases, what Revival was, was the church coming into true SALVATION for the first time. They THOUGHT they were saved before, but they had been under a delusion. When the 'Revivalist' arrived and preached to them, suddenly they saw that they were undone and in a lost state, and multitudes were converted. Revival almost always begins with the church.

As we have seen, with the hugely lukewarm state of today's Western church, it is very easy to believe that a large percentage of our churchgoers are not walking in a state of true New Testament salvation at all. One evangelical pastor told me that he thinks perhaps 5% or 10% of his congregation is truly saved. I can well believe it – and we need to multiply that by literally thousands of churches nationwide. Remember, church attendance in the US is quite high (over 35%). But everyone agrees that there is an enormous amount of 'nominal' Christianity and 'social' Christianity going on – as well as a large number of people who attend churches where they are told they are 'saved' when clearly they are not.

It is difficult not to come to the conclusion that many of these churches are like "holding pens" for the damned – telling people that they are 'OK', when in reality they are headed for destruction. Personally, I find this very hard to take. What will God do to the preachers who are lulling the flock to sleep in this way? And when will preachers be found who will dare to tell the "Christians" that most are not saved at all – but still in their sins? Such is the role of the true prophet of God. Such is the role of the coming "John the Baptists".

Of course, Finney was hated and despised by churchmen for saying such things. How DARE he preach in such a way that implied that many 'fine church members' were unsaved? How offensive and ill-mannered! But Finney had such a passion and a burden to REACH THE 'CHRISTIANS' with the gospel. And this was exactly what God had called him to do.

Today we see exactly the same thing in the West as Finney saw in his day. We see a "church" that is very largely UNSAVED. A truly "saved" church (in the New Testament sense) behaves and looks and sounds utterly different to what we see today.

Even in 'Spirit-filled' circles we often find many "previously-saved-but-no-longer-walking-in-it" believers. Friends, this is not a state of 'salvation'. The Bible is very clear that only those who CONTINUE in New Testament Christianity and who "overcome" will be saved. These people are lost. You are either walking as a 'new creature' filled with love for Christ or you are not. If you are not walking in it then do not assume you are "saved" – no matter what some preacher tells you. It is all or nothing with God. The Bible tells us to "work out our salvation with fear and trembling". I would be very surprised if more than a quarter of the West's so-called "Spirit-filled" believers are actually walking with a clean heart before God. What on earth do they think will happen to them on Judgment Day?

Added to this, we have millions upon millions of 'old mainline' believers who literally NEVER get the opportunity to find out about "FULL" salvation. The Holy Spirit is never made real to them, and many have never been fully BAPTIZED in water, either.

So how on earth do we reach all these vast millions who are being duped with this half-Christianity – and who never get to hear the full gospel? What on earth can be done to get this message through to them?

This is a burden that is very much on my heart. And I am convinced that only the coming "John-the-Baptist" ministries will have the anointing to break through the walls of 'Religion' to reach these people with the truth. We are talking about millions upon millions of precious souls here. And they are people who DO BELIEVE in God. But they have been lied-to, and the real truth has been denied them.

I am convinced that a vital part of the coming harvest must begin with the CHURCH. It must begin with converting the "CHRISTIANS". This has often been God's order. "First in Jerusalem, then in Judea...."

I am deeply burdened for the church in the West. Let the new Charles Finneys arise! Let the trumpet sound go forth! The message of PIERCING REPENTANCE must be heard in the land once again. And the idol of 'Mammon' must surely be one of it's key targets. "For the word of God is quick and powerful, sharper than any two-edged sword." May this mighty sword be brought to bear on the walls of Religion and false 'assurance' in our day.

A "GOSPEL" THAT IS NO GOSPEL

To follow on from the previous section, let me also make this statement: There is no tragedy in the world worse than this - the church losing the gospel. We could have a hundred terrorist attacks, or earthquakes, or hurricanes, and it would still not outweigh the tragedy of this one thing – THE CHURCH LOSING THE GOSPEL. Nothing can compare to this disaster – nothing.

For when you lose the gospel, you lose salvation. People are actually no longer becoming saved. (Remember, Paul said that the gospel is the "power of God unto salvation"). And when people are no longer truly becoming saved, you also lose the church. For no true gospel = no true church.

People will tell me that I am being too "drastic". Well, I want to say to you that I am not being drastic enough. In fact, if I were to shout through 1000 megaphones directly into your ears, it would not be possible for me to over-emphasize just how disastrous and awful and horrific it is that our backslidden Western church today has – to all intents and purposes – lost its gospel. And in doing so it has lost its very reason for being.

We tell everybody that all they need to do is say a little rote prayer accepting Jesus as their "personal savior". Tell me, where is such a thing in Scripture? Does such a thing even come close to existing? Can you recall even ONE person doing such a thing to become a Christian in the Bible? Did any of the Apostles in Acts ever say to someone, "Just repeat this little prayer after me"? Or "Quietly slip up your hand – no need for anyone to see"? Can you remember anyone in Scripture doing anything like that?

No, you can't. That is because nobody ever did. It is all a modern fabrication – a complete invention. This is no salvation at all. We act like people can safely forget about CONVICTION of sin and DEEP REPENTANCE and WATER-BAPTISM and getting FILLED with the Holy Spirit. Just "optional extras", eh? But look at 'Acts' and tell me – was there ever such a thing as real Christianity without these things? And what about getting a CLEAN CONSCIENCE (washed in the blood) and keeping it clean? Are we ever told how to walk in that today? To actually "walk" in the washing of the blood of Jesus? To be clean, to be utterly clean, to be "every whit" clean? (The most important thing in the world). Where is this in our gospel? Where is the transformed life? Where is the freedom from sin?

We have lost it all. Our people very rarely repent. They often go for years without baptism (meaning, according to Romans 6, that their "old man" is not yet dead – and so they simply cannot live a new life in Christ). Read Romans 6 sometime and ask yourself this question – "If I have not been baptized, then is my old life "buried" with Christ or not? Is my 'old man' dead or not?" This is why the apostles always baptized people IMMEDIATELY.

And then we often fail to get people filled with the Spirit right away too – let alone "walking" in the Spirit. Tell me, how are we supposed to have Holiness if we have not even been filled with the "HOLY" Spirit? Why do you think the apostles always made sure that people became Spirit-filled RIGHT AWAY?

Most of us do not even have "Day One" Christianity as it was in the Bible. We have lost the gospel and we don't even know it. We have invented a gospel of 'convenience', a gospel without the cross, a gospel without holiness or the power to live a Christian life. A gospel that shows no-one how to get a clean conscience or how to walk in it. I want to say to you that such a gospel is NO GOSPEL AT ALL. And we should be ashamed of ourselves for preaching such a travesty.

No wonder today's church is lukewarm! The gospel is the building block upon which everything else is built. Without it we have nothing – literally nothing. It affects all that we do and all that we are. To lose it is simply the worst disaster imaginable. So how on earth can we get it back?

Well, we have spoken about 'Revival' many times in this book. But one aspect that we haven't fully discussed is that the "Return of the Gospel" was often the key that brought about the Great Awakenings – the gospel being restored and preached in power once again. The longest-lasting Revivals always involved the "Return of the Gospel". That is precisely what was happening with the preaching of Wesley, Finney, Whitefield, etc. And it needs to happen again today!

So "Revival" to me is far more than just a fleeting visitation. It is to be the long-lasting restoration of the true gospel - and thus the true church also. If we want true Christianity restored today, we must first see the gospel restored. It is the most important key to it all. O God, send such a Revival! Bring back your true gospel and those who will preach it! O God, we cry out to you in the mighty name of Jesus... Amen.

THE FALSE DISCREDITS THE TRUE

As we saw earlier in this book when we were discussing counterfeits and false manifestations, etc, one of the major reasons that Satan uses counterfeits is to try and bring disgrace and discredit upon the REAL moving of the Holy Spirit. As John Wesley stated, these things "bring the real work into contempt." And I feel that this is exactly what has been going on with the Charismatic movement in recent times. The antics and falsehoods of a lot of Charismatic preachers have turned off entire sections of Christendom from seeking to be filled with the Holy Spirit or to receive true spiritual gifts, etc. And I think this is a terrible shame. For that is exactly what the devil wants. He wants everyone to take note only of the excesses and counterfeits – and thus to be turned off the real thing.

Please hear me in this: The baptism of the Holy Spirit is one of the most powerful and important experiences in God that you can ever have. It is completely biblical, and is regarded as totally essential by every Revivalist that I have ever read about. Personally, when I myself had this experience at the age of 17 years, it utterly transformed my life.

Let us take a look at Charles Finney's description of his own 'baptism in the Spirit', which occurred the day he was converted:

As I closed the door and turned around, my heart seemed to be liquid within me. All my feelings seemed to rise and flow out, and the cry of my heart was, "I want to pour my whole soul out to God." The intensity was so great that I rushed into the room behind the front office, to pray.

There was no fire and no light in the room, but it appeared to me as if it was perfectly light. As I went in and shut the door, it seemed like I met the Lord Jesus Christ face to face. It seemed to me that I saw Him as I would see any other man. He said nothing, but looked at me in a way that broke me right down at his feet. I poured out my soul to Him. I wept aloud like a child, and made whatever confessions I could. It seemed to me that I bathed His feet with my tears; and yet I had no distinct impression that I touched Him.

I must have continued this way for quite some time, but I was too absorbed to remember anything I said. I know that as soon as my mind became calm enough, I returned to the front office, and found that the fire was nearly burned out. But as I turned and was about to take a seat by the fire, I received a mighty baptism of the Holy Spirit. Without any expectation of it, without any thought in my mind that there was any such thing for me, the Holy Spirit descended upon me in a way that seemed to go through me, body and soul. It was like a wave of electricity, going through and through me. Indeed it seemed to come in waves and waves of liquid love. It seemed like the very breath of God. I remember distinctly that it seemed to fan me, like immense wings.

No words can express the wonderful love that filled my heart. I wept aloud with joy and love; I literally bellowed out the inexpressible floods of my heart. These waves came over me and over me, one after the other, until I cried out, "I will die if these waves continue." I said, "Lord, I cannot bear any more." Yet I had no fear of death. How long I continued in this state, with this baptism continuing to roll over me and go through me, I do not know. But I know it was late in the evening when a member of my choir - for I was the leader of the choir - came into the office to see me. He found me in this state of loud weeping, and said to me, "Mr. Finney, what's wrong?" I could not answer for some time. He then said, "Are you in pain?" I gathered myself up as best I could, and replied, "No, but so happy that I cannot live."

After this mighty baptism in the Holy Spirit, Finney found that wherever he went, his words pierced people with conviction of sin like an "arrow to the heart". Sometimes it was only necessary for him to speak a few words, and conviction came upon them. In many ways this was truly the day that he became a Revivalist.

I cannot say that my own baptism in the Spirit was as spectacular as Finney's, but it certainly transformed my life utterly in the space of just one day. I was 17 years old when it happened – and part of a Baptist church. Some Baptist friends of mine had been telling me about this experience – and I could see the huge difference it made in their lives. I began to seek God a lot more, repenting of my sins and surrendering my whole life to Him. But I knew that I needed to find someone to pray for me to receive this baptism of the Spirit. God led me to a young Christian leader whom I knew was Spirit-filled, and I asked him to "lay hands" on me and pray for me to be filled with the Holy Spirit. What a transformation! To this day, I still believe it was the most powerful experience of my life. I was transformed instantly into a different person. The glory of God filled my very being. And the next day I spoke in tongues for the first time – just like we see in the Bible. But the most incredible part for me was that I was suddenly filled with the love, the power and the glory of God. And 'holiness' was the major fruit in my life

– for I had been filled with God's "HOLY" Spirit – and He is the Spirit of holiness. That was 24 years ago now and I can tell you – the change was permanent. It really was the most transforming experience of my life. So if you are yet to experience this, then make it a priority, my friends. Do not rest until God has baptized you "with the Holy Spirit and with fire."

I know that a lot of people today have all kinds of objections to "tongues" and other things. As I said before, I believe a lot of this is caused by seeing the excesses and falsehoods of many Charismatic preachers today. This has turned a huge number of people off – it really has. But you can't let these excesses rob you of such a vital, wonderful and utterly biblical experience in God – you really can't. This is too important to let the devil steal it away from you.

The fact is, 'tongues' and "laying on of hands" are found right through the New Testament. And in the book of Acts we see them time and time again – when people are being filled with the Holy Spirit (see Acts 2, Acts 8, Acts 10 & 11, Acts 19, etc). This is a very important biblical experience, and if you hope to be part of any kind of Revival – or even just basic New Testament Christianity – then it really is a must.

"But who should I get to lay hands on me?" you may ask. Well, there are many simple Pentecostal fellowships today where they are not into weird excesses, but would be happy to pray for you. If you can't find a place like that, then simply seek God alone at home. Pray and pray, surrendering all to Him, and ask Him to fill you to overflowing with His Spirit, His power, His love and His holiness. "Not by might, not by power, but by my Spirit, says the Lord."

"But should I definitely expect to speak in tongues?" you may ask. The simple answer is: "Yes, you should!" We not only have the biblical record telling us that people spoke in tongues when they were filled, but we also have 100 years of Pentecostal history now, in which literally hundreds of millions of people around the world have received this experience. (The vast majority of Revivals happening in Third World countries today are of this 'Pentecostal' type).

"But why tongues?" you may ask. Well, tongues is a sign that "utterance" has been given to you by the Holy Spirit. It is a sign that the word of God is now in your mouth – that God is truly able to 'take over' your tongue and speak through you. And very importantly it is also a personal 'prayer language' that you can use to pray to God. This is why the apostle Paul said, "I speak with tongues more than you all" (1 Cor 14:18). Paul was obviously spending a good part of each day praying in tongues. And I have learnt to do this myself – especially when I have a preaching engagement coming up. (I have heard of other preachers who find this very powerful also). I have found that when I pray for some hours in tongues, when I get up to preach there is a much stronger sense of the holy presence of God and the word goes forth with convicting power. I believe this is a very under-used gift in the body of Christ, and a real secret to ministering in the power of the Holy Spirit. So I strongly urge everyone to spend a lot more time praying in tongues.

As we noted earlier, the Holy Spirit is a Spirit of holiness. His very essence is "holy". If you see something that is unholy, then it is not coming from the Holy Spirit. It is true that God may do strange or unusual things at times – and there really can be a joyful freedom and liberty exhibited in Christ which can be quite startling. But if you see things that are weird or ugly or unholy, then you know it is not of Him. Our God is a God of holiness – and His "Holy" Spirit likewise. He simply does not go against His own character.

IN CONCLUSION

In this book, we have looked at true and false manifestations – and how to tell the difference. We have looked at the essence of what true Revival is – primarily GETTING DEEPLY RIGHT WITH GOD, and also becoming filled with His Spirit of 'HOLINESS'.

We have also looked at how badly we need TRUE PROPHETS in this generation – and the kind of piercing message they will bring. We have looked at how compromise brought forth deception, and deception brought forth invasion. Yet God is still in control.

We are in a time of testing and separation. There is an end-time "sifting" going on amongst the people of God. That is why the Lord is allowing this invasion. Out of all this shaking and dividing He will bring forth a purified and set-apart Bride – "without spot or wrinkle or any such thing". Strange fire is not to be offered on the altar of God. This is a separating of the holy from the profane. It is a testing of hearts. And the Lord is deliberately allowing it. Will you pass the test, my friend?

God is looking for a people who will "wait" and not run after Ishmael. This has been one of the greatest causes for the rise of the False in this hour – men who could not WAIT for God. They preferred to run after false fire than to pay the price and wait for the true. And oh – how they will come to regret their hastiness.

There is another thing that I believe is about to plunge the Western church into the fires of trial and purging also: It is a great economic depression. I believe God will use this to drive the "love of money" out of the church. No longer will the worship of Mammon co-exist side-by-side with the worship of Christ in the church. A great separation is coming. The idol of Mammon is coming down. The money-changers will be driven forcibly out of the temple. And this will bring about even greater separation between the true and the false.

These two events – the rise of great Last Days deception alongside great financial crisis – will bring testing and purging to the church on an unprecedented scale. Judgment truly begins at the house of God – and my friends it is beginning NOW. Everything that can be shaken will be shaken. A great dividing is upon us. And God is going to use all of this to bring one last 'Great Reformation' to His church.

TWO REVIVALS?

There have been a number of prophecies over the years that speak of "two Revivals" coming in the Last Days – one big and popular, soulish and shallow – while the other is smaller yet full of holiness, truth and love. Could these Revivals take place almost side by side? I believe this is very possible. In fact, I believe it is to be expected.

Some may think that because the picture I have painted in this book is so terrible regarding the state of the Western church, that perhaps I have "lost hope" for real Revival in this generation. This is not the case at all. I still have tremendous hope for Revival.

I truly believe that God can still find His Finneys and Wesleys in this late hour – a true company of John-the-Baptists. I think there are many who have "not bowed the knee to Baal." They are hidden in the wildernesses and the caves, waiting for the hour of their showing forth. As we have seen, such preachers MUST be found if we are to see real Revival in this generation. All we can do is pray and pray that God will find them and raise them up before it is too late.

I believe it is very possible that we stand today at the beginning of the greatest "shaking", the greatest Reformation, and the greatest moving of God in the history of the church. Surely, for many, this will be the church's finest hour. But it will also be the hour of greatest peril. Many who looked to have the greatest potential will be found to have fallen at the final hurdle, or to have shrunk back from taking their ultimate stand with God. It is only those who are prepared and praying who will have a part in true Awakening.

The Scripture, "Many that are first will be last, and many that are last will be first," will come into play at every level in this Revival – even in the order of NATIONS. For as always, God will use the little and the foolish things of this world to confound the wise, the powerful and the mighty. There is coming a great tidal-wave of "CHANGE". The old order is about to be overthrown, and the 'new' is to be established by God. He is about to wrest back control of His church by force.

Sadly, in many ways the current situation reminds me very much of the parable of the 'wise and foolish virgins'. When those who were truly ready had entered in, the door was slammed shut, and the unprepared were locked out of the very marriage that they were supposed to be a part of. No wonder there was "wailing and gnashing of teeth"! We are about to see this parable quite literally fulfilled in our day. Tragically, like Esau, it seems clear that many in these times are going to be found to have sold their birthright for a mere "mess of pottage".

If we are truly close to the end of the age, then surely we live in the most momentous and yet dangerous days in the history of the church. How we respond to the opportunities and the dangers of this time is entirely over to us. I believe that we are about to see an army of preachers arise who will bring down many of Satan's strongholds of sin and compromise – both in the church and in the world – and who will go forth, 'destroying the works of the devil' in Jesus' name, with great daring and resolve.

It is truly time for the John-the-Baptists to come forth – hidden and prepared by God for years for this last, dark hour. I believe that the Lord is about to once again be seen as a 'God of war', shaking the nations and scattering His enemies to the dust. As I said, everything that can be shaken will be shaken. And Jesus Christ will gain for himself a glorious bride that is truly "without spot or wrinkle or any such thing."

No longer will God's people operate from a mindset of expecting the world to come to them. Rather, it will be God's people who will be going out into "all the world". And they will not be making mere 'church-goers' of all nations, but rather true DISCIPLES OF JESUS CHRIST. This will be their heart and their passion. And they will risk everything to accomplish it. These will be a people far more concerned with 'holiness' than with happiness. For them, true happiness will consist of walking in the very center of God's will. Glory to God!

I believe there is very strong call going forth in our day. It is a call to preachers to forsake their fear of man, their security, their reputation. It is a call to every Christian to unprecedented boldness, recklessness and agonizing prayer. It is a call to the cross – to the laying down of all. It is a call to the place of "no reputation." Tell me, friend, is this you? Will you be a "truth-teller" in the midst of a generation that increasingly loves and embraces lies? Remember, true prophets are not just known for standing up for truth – but also for standing against the false.

My prayer is that, in some small way, this book will help to warn and prepare all who read it for the momentous days ahead, so that as many as possible might become part of God's true move. There is a dividing taking place – a separation. But nevertheless His name is about to be glorified in all the earth. And He is inviting many of us to be a part of it – to become one of His "mighty men and women of valor" in this present hour. Friend, will you be one who heeds His call? Will you be one who marches to a different drum? Which do you choose at the end of the day – the narrow path of the true or the easy way of the false? I leave you to ponder the answer in your own heart.

VISIT OUR WEBSITE-

www.revivalschool.com

QUOTES AND REFERENCES

CHAPTER TWO.

1. 'PW' & 'Lynn' quotes - www.revivalschool.com
2. Todd Bentley, 'Angelic Hosts' - www.etpv.org/2003/angho.html
3. Todd Bentley, 'A Face To Face Encounter' – Part 2 - www.freshfire.ca
4. Missionary quote – Josef Urban - www.cristianismobiblico.com/bentleyexposed.htm
5. Todd Bentley on CBN News – www.cbnnews.com
6. UK Report – 'Dudley Outpouring' ~ http://www.supernaturalliving.com/welcome.html
7. J. Lee Grady, "Honest Questions About the Lakeland Revival", May 14, 2008 – www.charismamag.com/fireinmybones
8. Robert Walker quote -www.pastornet.net.au/response/articles/107.htm
9. Shri Yogãnandji Mahãrãja source: 'Devatma Shakti (Kundalini): Divine Power' by Swami Vishnu Tirtha - www.cit-sakti.com/kundalini/kundalini-manifestations.htm

10. Elijah List – www.elijahlist.com

CHAPTER THREE.

1. F. Bartleman, "Azusa Street", pg 19.
2. Source: Eifion Evans, "When He is Come", pg 55.
3. Source: F. Bartleman, "Azusa Street", pg 34-35.
4. "The Autobiography of Charles G. Finney" - condensed & edited by Helen Wessel, pg 82.
5. F. Bartleman, "Azusa Street", pg 69-70.
6. Evan Roberts. Source: David Matthews, "I Saw the Welsh Revival", pg 81.
7. A.W. Tozer. Introduction, L. Ravenhill, "Why Revival Tarries", pg 11-12. Copyright (c) 1959. Published by Bethany House. Used by permission.
8. D'Aubigne, "History of the Reformation". Source: F. Bartleman, "Azusa Street", pg 101-102.

9. Source: F. Bartleman, "Azusa Street", pg 46.
10. Humphrey Jones. Source: Eifion Evans, "When He is Come", pg 49.
11. Martin Luther. Source: L. Ravenhill, "Revival - God's Way", pg 15.
12. "The Autobiography of Charles G. Finney" - condensed & edited by Helen Wessel, pg 57.
13. Jonathan Edwards. Source: W. Pratney, "Revival", pg 117.
14. Source: Fischer, "Reviving Revivals", pg 84-86.
15. "The Autobiography of Charles G. Finney" - condensed & edited by Helen Wessel, pg 105.
16. F. Bartleman, "Azusa Street", pg 33.
17. D.M. McIntyre. Source: L. Ravenhill, "Why Revival Tarries", pg 16.
18. Matthew Henry. Source: Ibid. pg 26.
19. L. Ravenhill, "Why Revival Tarries", pg 42. Copyright (c) 1959. Published by Bethany House. Used by permission.
20. A.T Pierson. Source: Ibid. pg 156.
21. John Wesley. Source: Ibid. pg 16.
22. C.G. Finney. Source: Ibid. pg 150.
23. Jonathan Edwards. Source: Fischer, "Reviving Revivals", pg 158.
24. R.M. McCheyne. Source: L. Ravenhill, "Why Revival Tarries", pg 33.
25. F. Bartleman, "Azusa Street", pg 81.
26. Ibid. pg 43.
27. A. Booth-Clibborn. Source: Ibid. pg 55.

CHAPTER FOUR.

1. F. Bartleman, "Azusa Street", pg 152.
2. John Wesley. Source: F. Bartleman, "Azusa Street", pg 45.
3. John Wesley. Source: G. Strachan, "Revival - It's Blessings and Battles", pg 44.
4. John Wesley. Source: F. Bartleman, "Azusa Street", pg 45.
5. C.G. Finney, "Reflections on Revival", pg 66.
6. F. Bartleman, "Azusa Street", pg 86.
7. "Jonathan Edwards on Revival", pg 153-154.
8. "The Journal of John Wesley", April 3, 1786.
9. George Lavington - www.christianword.org/revival/rissman1.html
10. Boston Evening Post, ~1743.
11. Keith J. Hardman, "The Spiritual Awakeners", pg 138.
12. T.W. Caskey. Source: "Seventy years in Dixie" by F.D. Srygley.
13. Steve Turner, "Hungry for Heaven".

14. J. Penn-Lewis, "War on the Saints", pg 150-151.
15. J. Penn-Lewis, "War on the Saints", pg 148.

CHAPTER FIVE.

1. CBN News Report - www.cbn.com , Jan 6, 2002.
2. Dana Candler, "Deep Unto Deep - The Journey of the Embrace", pg 57, 52, 84.
3. 'Bridegroom Fast' quote - www.sermonindex.net

CHAPTER SIX.

1. Leonard Ravenhill, "Why Revival Tarries", pg 104-105.
2. A.G. Gardiner - Source: A. Wallis, "In the Day of Thy Power", pg 81.
3. Leonard Ravenhill, "Why Revival Tarries", pg 39.
4. Finney sermon - Source: "The Memoirs of Charles Finney", pg 100.

CHAPTER SEVEN.

1. J. Lee Grady, "Fire in my Bones", July 27, 2007 - www.charismamag.com/fireinmybones
2. J. Lee Grady, "Fire in my Bones" June 9, 2006 - www.charismamag.com/fireinmybones
3. "Charles Finney Revivalist - edited and updated", pg 11.

Printed in the United States
117248LV00004B/319-348/P